Prestel Museum Guide

Alte Pinakothek
Munich

By
Martin Schawe

Prestel
Munich · London · New York

Bayerische Staatsgemäldesammlungen
Alte Pinakothek Munich
Barer Straße 27
(entrance on Theresienstraße)
80333 Munich
Phone: 089 / 2 38 05-2 16
Fax: 089 / 2 38 05-2 21

Photos: page 9 bottom, 17, 20, 21, 23, 24/25, 29, 34 bottom, 35, 41 bottom,
42, 49–52, 53 bottom, 57, 59, 64, 68, 69 bottom, 71 bottom, 72 bottom, 74,
76 top, 77, 83, 85 bottom, 86, 88 top, 92 bottom, 93, 96 bottom, 98, 103 top,
106, 110, 112 top, 118, 121 bottom, 122–124, 138 top: Artothek, Peißenberg
All other illustrations were taken from the archives of the Bayerische Staatsgemälde-
sammlungen

Front cover: Peter Paul Rubens, *Rubens and Isabella Brant in a Honeysuckle Bower*,
c. 1609, detail from ill. p. 76
Back cover: The exterior of the Alte Pinakothek
Photo: Jens Weber

The Publisher would like to thank Artothek for kindly providing pictorial material for this
guidebook

Prestel Verlag
Mandlstraße 26, D-80802 Munich, Germany
Tel. +49 (89) 38 17 09-0, Fax +49 (89) 38 17 09-35;
4 Bloomsbury Place, London WC1A 2QA
Tel. +44 (0171) 323-5004, Fax +44 (0171) 636-8004;
and 16 West 22nd Street, New York, NY 10010, USA
Tel. (212) 627-8199, Fax (212) 627-9866

Prestel books are available worldwide.
Please contact your nearest bookseller or write to one of the above addresses for information
concerning your local distributor.

Library of Congress Cataloging-in-Publication Data is available for this title.

Translated from the German by Joan Clough
Copyedited by Dona Geyer
Designed by Verlagsservice G. Pfeifer, Germering
Lithography by Repro Line, Munich
Printed and bound by Passavia Druckservice GmbH, Passau

Printed in Germany on acid-free paper

ISBN 3-7913-2230-7

Contents

History of the Collection

The Alte Pinakothek is part of the Bayerische Staatsgemälde-sammlungen (the Bavarian State Collections of Paintings), which comprises four museums in Munich: the Alte and the Neue Pinakothek, the Staatsgalerie moderner Kunst and the Schack-Galerie. In addition, there are 15 Staatsgalerien (State Galleries) throughout Bavaria. The administration of all these museums, overseeing roughly 30,000 works of art in Bavaria, is housed in a wing of the Neue Pinakothek. Some of the branch galleries had to be established as early as the 19th century to take the overflow from the four Munich collections. Consequently, numerous Early German paintings are hung in Aschaffenburg, Augsburg, Bamberg, Burghausen, Füssen and Ottobeuren. There are Baroque paintings in Ansbach, Kulmbach, Schleissheim and Würzburg.

The major factor determining acquisitions policy in the Bayerische Staatsgemäldesammlungen collections was the active commitment to acquiring paintings shown by the former rulers of the State of Bavaria. The collection does indeed express the personal preferences of the individual rulers. However, the disjointed process of acquisition over a long period of time has also made it possible to keep unique groupings of works together. The collection reflects the turbulent history of the House of Wittelsbach; extinction of royal lines, bequests, merging of inventories and shifts in emphasis have all left their mark on the Alte Pinakothek to make it the world-class art museum it is today.

1528/40 The groundwork of the present Alte Pinakothek collection was laid by Duke Wilhelm IV of Bavaria (1493–1550) and his wife, Jacobaea von Baden (1507–1580), who commissioned a series of history paintings for the Munich Residenz, among them Altdorfer's *Battle of Issus*.

1563–1567 The Kunstkammer (later 'Mint') was built by Wilhelm Egkl in the reign of Duke Albrecht V (1528–1579). An inventory drawn up in 1598 lists some 778 paintings.

1597–1651 The Prince Elector Maximilian I (1573–1651) acquired major Old German paintings, including Albrecht Dürer's *Four Apostles*, and had them hung in the Kammergalerie established in 1611–1617. He commissioned Peter Paul Rubens to paint a hunting cycle in 1615/16 for Schleissheim Castle. Only the *Hippopotamus Hunt* is still in Munich. Concurrently, another Wittelsbach, Wolfgang Wilhelm, Count Palatine of Neuburg, Jülich and Berg (1578–1653), commissioned Rubens to paint the altarpiece for the high altar of the Jesuit church in Neuburg on the

Danube, the *Large Last Judgement*, which later went to Munich.

1679–1726 The Prince Elector Maximilian II Emanuel (1662–1726) continued to add to his grandfather's collection. In 1698, while Stadholder of the Netherlands, he acquired 101 Flemish paintings from the collection owned by the Antwerp merchant Gisbert van Colen. Among these were 12 paintings by Rubens, which today are among the most important works in the Alte Pinakothek. Over 1000 paintings were hung in new Schleissheim Castle. At about the same time, the Prince Elector Johann Wilhelm of the Palatinate (1658–1716), a grandson of Wolfgang Wilhelm of the Palatinate-Neuburg, was amassing a superb collection of Italian and Flemish masterpieces in his seat at Düsseldorf. All these paintings later found their way to Munich.

1777 The Bavarian Line of the House of Wittelsbach became extinct. The Prince Elector Karl Theodor of the Palatinate (1724–1799) inherited all the Bavarian and Palatinate demesnes.

1780/81 Karl Theodor commissioned the Hofgartengalerie above the northern Hofgarten arcades (1613–1617), built by Maximilian. Afraid that the French armies approaching Mannheim might steal the 758 paintings in the Mannheim Gallery, he had them brought to Munich in 1798. Most of these were 17th-century Dutch and Flemish, among them major work by Jan Brueghel and Rembrandt's *The Sacrifice of Isaac*.

1799–1825 Karl Theodor's death ended the Palatinate Wittelsbach line. On his accession to the Bavarian throne, the Prince Elector Maximilian IV Joseph (1756–1825, from 1806 King Max I Joseph) of the Palatinate-Zweibrücken line incorporated the Zweibrücken gallery of paintings in the Munich collection. This important collection comprised at least 2000 works: Early German, Flemish, Dutch and later French paintings, among them Chardin's *Woman Cleaning Turnips* and Boucher's *Reclining Girl*.

1800 The invading French confiscated paintings and took them to Paris. By 1815 only 27 had been returned; 45 remained in France.

From 1803 the era of secularization saw 1500 paintings returned to Munich, among them important Early German altarpieces. Branch galleries were established in Augsburg, Ansbach, Bamberg, Würzburg, Nuremberg and Aschaffenburg.

From 1805 The Crown Prince and later King Ludwig I (1786–1868) acquired numerous Italian paintings, among them works by Giotto, Botticelli, Filippino Lippi, Domenico Ghirlandaio, Perugino and Raphael. By the inauguration of the Alte Pinakothek in 1836, Ludwig had assembled 97 of the 314 paintings now comprising the Italian Section, all of them major works.

1806 The Düsseldorf gallery of paintings belonging to Johann Wilhelm of the Palatinate, already bequeathed to Karl Theodor in 1777, was transferred to Munich.

1826 The cornerstone of the (Alte) Pinakothek was laid (architect: Leo von Klenze) on 7 April, Raphael's birthday.

1827 King Ludwig I acquired for Munich the 216 pictures comprising the Boisserée Collection for 240,000 guilders: South German and Cologne paintings by the Master of the Life of the Virgin and Stefan Lochner; and, most importantly, major works by the Early Netherlandish School: Rogier van der Weyden's *Columba Altar*, Dieric Bouts' *Pearl of Brabant* and Hans Memling's *Seven Joys of the Virgin*.

1828 King Ludwig I bought 219 Old German Master paintings of the Swabian, Franconian, Central and South German Schools from the Oettingen-Wallerstein Collection for 80,000 guilders, among them Dürer's *Oswolt Krel* and Aldorfer's *Danube Landscape*.

1836 Inauguration of the (Alte) Pinakothek.

1838 First catalogue of paintings published (Dillis).

1939–1945 The Alte Pinakothek closed for the duration of the war. The paintings were stored at first in Munich, then moved in 1942 outside the city so that almost all were saved. Bombing raids on 9 March 1943, 25 April, 12 and 16 July and 17 December 1944 severely damaged the building.

1946–1957 Paintings from the Alte Pinakothek and the then Neue Staatsgalerie (corresponding to the inventory of later paintings from 1850 in the Neue Pinakothek) were hung in the Haus der Kunst.

1952–1957 The Alte Pinakothek was rebuilt by Hans Döllgast. Traces of wartime damage have been left on the outer walls. They, as well as the vast staircase on the south side (it once housed a spacious loggia in the upper storey, with the main entrance originally in the east wing), now enjoy historic monument status.

1957 On 7 June the Alte Pinakothek opened to the public again. In 1961 the lower floor in the east wing was inaugurated and in 1963 the lower floor of the west wing.

From 1966 works dating from the 18th century were on loan from the Bayerische Hypotheken- und Wechselbank, including Lancret's *Volière* and Boucher's *Mme de Pompadour*.

1977–1980 The roof was repaired and the gallery wall was resurfaced to comply with fire regulations.

1990 Dieric Bouts' *Ecce agnus dei* was acquired.

1994 On 5 April the Alte Pinakothek was closed for a general overhaul. A selection of paintings went on exhibit on 18 June in the Neue Pinakothek.

1998 On 23 July the Alte Pinakothek reopened.

Early Netherlandish Painting

In the early 15th century, art in the southern Netherlands suddenly took a quantum leap in its development. Franco-Flemish manuscript illumination led to highly sophisticated techniques of panel painting, distinguished by microscopic naturalism in detail and glowing colour. Campin, the van Eyck brothers, van der Weyden, Bouts and Memling attracted a clientele of merchants and traders who travelled to far-flung outposts, rich burghers and clergy as well as members of royal and ducal courts who commissioned portraits of themselves and pictures for their private devotions or invested money in art for the salvation of their own souls and to the glory of the Church. Early Netherlandish painting exerted an enormous influence on the art of neighbouring countries and was appreciated by connoisseurs even in Italy. For its size, the collection of Early Netherlandish paintings owned by the Alte Pinakothek boasts some supremely important works, most of them acquired in 1827 by King Ludwig I of Bavaria from the Boisserée Collection.

Rogier van der Weyden
(1399/1400 Tournai – 1464 Brussels)

Columba Altar, c. 1455

Panel, 138 x ca. 293 cm (overall) – inv. no.
WAF 1189-WAF 1191 – Acquired in 1827
from the Boisserée Collection

The Columba Altar is a highlight
of the Alte Pinakothek collection
and a major work of Early
Netherlandish art. The Adoration
of the Magi, the Annunciation
and the Presentation in the Tem-
ple, eight days after Christ's
birth, are represented on the central panel and wings. Glowing
colour and microscopic fineness
of detail as well as the solemnity
the figures radiate impressed
Goethe when he spent a long
time gazing at the work in Hei-
delberg in 1814/15. Cryptic details
like the Crucified hanging above
the newborn Child, the relief of
the Fall of Man on the Virgin's
prayer stool in The Annunciation
and 'New Eve', astonishingly
reveal profound theological
thought. The Columba Altar is
named after its provenance: the
Goedert van den Wasserfass
chapel in the Cologne church of
St Columba. However, it is not
known whether the altarpiece

was originally made for the chapel. The donor represented
remains unknown.

Dieric Bouts
(1410/20 Haarlem – 1475 Louvain)

'Ecce agnus dei', c. 1462/64

Panel, 53.8 x 41.2 cm – inv. no. 15192 –
Acquired in 1990 through the support of
the Kulturstiftung der Länder

A religious attitude is expressed
in visual terms here; the kneeling
donor claims to be living according to Christ's teachings. A (his
patron?) saint, John the Baptist,
is standing at his side to succour
him. The focal point of the representation is the Bible. St John's
demonstrative gesture alludes to
the words 'Behold the Lamb of
God' (John I, 29 and 36) which
he preached on the River Jordan,
inspiring the first disciples to follow Christ (John I, 37). Both
dividing and unifying, the river
signifies that Christ is only
reached through baptism. This
frame of reference was obvious
to medieval viewers of the painting. Further, they would have rec-
ognized the symbolic significance, the allusions to Christ,

Dieric Bouts
(1410/20 Haarlem – 1475 Louvain)

Hinged altarpiece ('The Pearl of Brabant'), c. 1465

Panel, 62.6 x ca 117.6 cm (overall) – inv. nos. WAF 76, WAF 77, WAF 78 – Acquired in 1827 from the Boisserée Collection

The name sounds romantic but has only been recorded since the early 20th century. It refers to the jewel-like radiance of this little altar as well as the lively descriptive scenes illustrating the times of day on the wings: John the Baptist in the morning light on the left wing and St Christopher (Greek: the bearer of Christ) in the evening light on the right. The landscape depicted on the left-hand panel invites comparison with the Bouts' *Ecce agnus dei*. On the outer panels of the wings there are representations in grisaille of Saints Catherine and Barbara. Because it is so small, this altar was probably used in private devotions.

the Tree of Life, the numerous semiprecious stones scattered in the water and on the river bank. Extraordinary delicacy of handling make this painting one of the artist's undisputed masterpieces. It is the most recent and most important work to have been acquired by the Early Netherlandish Section since the Alte Pinakothek was founded. In a replica of the painting (in Berlin), the donor has been replaced by the listeners mentioned in the Bible passage.

Hans Memling

(Seligenstadt am Main c. 1435/40 –
Bruges 1494)

The Seven Joys of the Virgin, 1480

Panel, 81 x 189 cm – inv. no. WAF 668 –
Acquired in 1827 from the Boisserée
Collection

The title traditionally used for this
painting is inappropriate, for what
Memling has represented with
miniature-like precision is not
(unmitigated) joy. Not seven, but at
least twenty-five scenes make up
this unusually wide landsc.pe format. One must imagine the panel
as an opened hinged altarpiece. At
the centre the story of the Three
Kings or Magi is represented: taking their bearings from the star
above the three mountains in the
background; their three splendid
retinues converging, the adoration

of the Christ Child in the foreground and the opulent return pro-
cession taking a different route to
avoid encountering Herod's min-
ions and revealing the Child's
whereabouts to them. The second
'thread of the discourse' is the story
of the Virgin, in the left-hand quarter of the representation, from the
Annunciation through the birth of
Christ and the miraculous Flight
into Egypt. In the right-hand quarter, Christ after the Resurrection,
his Ascension into Heaven and,
finally, the Pentecost miracle are
depicted. The overarching theme of
the "Life of Christ" – from the time
before his birth to after his death –
subsumes nearly all the other
scenes. This is why the three Magi,
whose feast is celebrated on 6 January as Epiphany (manifestation),
are at the centre and why the

Descent of the Holy Ghost has been positioned so importantly. The Pentecost miracle marked the beginning of the Church. The painting was commissioned in 1480 for the Tanners' Guild chapel in the Church of Our Lady in Bruges. The donor, Pieter Bultync, is depicted with his son on the left and his wife, Katharina van Riebeke on the right.

Jean Hay
(active in Burgundy between c. 1480 and 1500)

Charles II de Bourbon, c. 1480/85
Panel, 34 x 25 cm – inv. no. WAF 648 – Acquired in 1827 from the Boisserée Collection

Charles II de Bourbon (1434-1488), the son of Duke Charles I of Burgundy, entered the Church: in 1447

he was Archbishop of Lyon; in 1465 Papal nuncio and in 1476, when he had his portrait painted, he was anointed Cardinal. The panel painting was probably part of a diptych.

Gerard David

*(Oudewater near Gouda
c. 1460 – Bruges 1523)*

Adoration of the Magi, c. 1495

Panel, 123 x 166 cm – inv. no. 715 –
Acquired in 1816 from a private collection
in Paris

David represents the generation of painters in Bruges after Memling. He, too, has chosen The Adoration of the Magi, the principal motif in late medieval painting (see the *Columba Altar* or the *Pearl of Brabant*), as his subject. In his composition, David follows a lost Hugo van der Goes. However, drawing on the life of his times, David has placed the principal figures in a lively pictorial context with peasant figures which are not simply staffage. Joseph, often rendered in late medieval painting as an elderly man, has seldom been represented with such quiet dignity as here, as a fresh-faced young father. Like Joseph, the African figures have been reticently depicted as real people. The Virgin is seated, with the Christ Child on her lap, before the ruins of King David's once splendid palace. Rapt in thought, the Virgin might also be seen as an isolated enthroned figure, for the infant Christ is turned toward us rather than toward his generous visitors. The Kings approach him with veneration, not regally as in the *Columba Altar*, but hesitantly as if afraid to enter the sacred precincts, which are clearly demarcated by a steep threshold behind them. The device of the crumbled wall divides the composition into two parts. The only linking element is the wheat sheaf in the foreground. In alluding to the doctrine of Transubstantion, the conversion of bread and wine in the Eucharist, it celebrates the birth of Christ. Indeed, the entire composition is suffused with the sacrament of the Eucharist, which mediates between God and man.

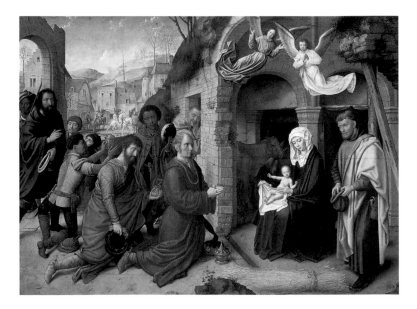

Lucas van Leyden
*(Leiden, presumably 1494 –
Leiden 1533)*

The Virgin and Child with St Mary Magdalene and a Donor, 1522

Panel, 50.5 x 67.8 cm – monogrammed
and dated – inv. no. 742 – Acquired
before 1628

This is a painting which looks
back on a turbulent history.
Before 1604 it was acquired by
the Emperor Rudolf II from the
Frans Hooghstraet collection
(near Leiden). A few years later it
is recorded in the Kammergalerie
of the Prince Elector Maximilian I
in Munich. By this time the two
panels, originally semicircular at
the top, had been fused and additions had made them one high
rectangular panel. Moreover, the
addition of attributes (the lily and
carpenters' tools) had turned the
kneeling donor into a St Joseph,
not an isolated instance of iconographic change at the time. In

1911 most of the iconographic
additions to the panel were re-
moved. Until 1874, there was an
Annunciation (now detached) on
the back. In this, his earliest
dated painting, van Leyden was
inspired by Venetian models as
well as Albrecht Dürer's graphic
work, which he had seen a few
months previously in Antwerp.

Jan Gossaert, called Mabuse
*(Maubeuge in Hainault,
c. 1478 – Breda 1532)*

Danae, 1527

Panel, 113.5 x 95 cm – signed and dated –
inv. no. 38 – presumably from the collection of the Emperor Rudolf II; from 1748
recorded in the Prince Elector's Gallery.

The choice of subject matter from
ancient mythology and an architectural setting in the antique
manner clearly indicate that this
is a Renaissance work. Gossaert
was the first Early Netherlandish

painter to assimilate and use what he had learnt from experiencing Italian painting and ancient art firsthand in Italy, where he stayed in Rome with Philip of Burgundy in 1508/09. Here the risqué story is told of how Zeus, the father of the gods, approached the daughter of the King of Argos as a shower of gold. In the Middle Ages the myth stood for chastity being corrupted by gold. Gossaert's unusual approach to the story has been viewed as drawing on this earlier tradition. Gossaert's depiction looks like a Christian version of the myth. The niche with its framing element at the top more closely resembles a shrine than a building. The overall effect is not without erotic connotations. The graceful figure evokes nudity by pulling up her skirt. Her legs are suggestively wide apart and she is looking up in expectation. All these racy details coupled with a coolly metallic cast of colour make this a delightful cabinet picture for connoisseurs.

Early German Painting

German 15th-century painting is for the most part anonymous and regionally diverse. Works are grouped under 'convenience names' ('Master of ...'). Not until the late 15th century do we begin to encounter artists as individuals. With Dürer, Cranach and Altdorfer, German art takes on definitive contours. Art is still largely religious in content and purpose. Hinged altarpieces could be opened or closed to display representations as the Church calendar demanded. Smaller versions of these were used for private devotions. Funerary representations commemorate the dead. Museums can only hint how these works functioned in their original contexts. The earliest portraits of this period are of the donors who commissioned the paintings. Then, in the Renaissance, supremely self-confident merchants and nobles look out at us from individualized portraits. The subject matter of history paintings was diversified and for the first time works were commissioned as collector's items. In the early 17th and 19th centuries, the Wittelsbach passion for art collecting and secularization made the Early German paintings collection what it is today.

Master of St Veronica

(active in Cologne 1st quarter of the 15th century)

St Veronica, c. 1420

Panel, 78.1 x 48.2 cm – inv. no. 11866 –
Acquired in 1827 from the Boisserée
Collection

Several versions of the true image of Christ were venerated during the Middle Ages. They were widespread in the form of pilgrim's badges and other artefacts. Legends explaining their miraculous origins and powers were believed to authenticate them. One legend, which goes back to about 1300, is related of St Veronica (vera icon = true image) giving a cloth to Christ on his way to Calvary so that he might wipe the sweat from his face. His face, with blood trickling down it, was imprinted on the cloth as a true image. The legend refers to a relic in Rome, which has drawn millions of pilgrims to St Peter's, where it is kept. Veneration of St Veronica and the sudarium ('sweat cloth') was linked with dispensations and hymns were written about them. The format of the painting and even the proportions of the figures portrayed are subordinated to its overarching thematic content: the true image of Christ.

Stefan Lochner

(Meersburg c. 1410 – Cologne 1451)

Adoration of the Virgin (Nativity), 1445

Panel, 37.5 x 23.6 cm – inv. no. 13169 –
Transferred from the state collection in 1961

Stefan Lochner is one of the earliest German artists whose name is linked with specific works. The Adoration of the Magi painted by 'maister steffans' and now in Cologne Cathedral was legendary even by the time it astonished Dürer in Cologne Town Hall.

Lochner's work represents an attractive synthesis of the Upper Rhenish, Netherlandish and Cologne traditions. This little painting is dominated by the figure of the Virgin, kneeling in worship before the Christ Child. Her dress is represented by a sophisticated swirl of crisp folds. A subordinate scene, The Annunciation to the Shepherds, opens up a deep landscape vista. Clusters of delicate, child-like angels, Lochner's hallmark, watch over the devotional scene, singing hymns. The overall impression is one of almost liturgical solemnity. The doctrinal content is the sacrament of the Eucharist. The Christ Child is lying on a cloth decorated with crosses, resembling the corporal on which the Communion wafer is laid during mass. Painted on both sides (a Crucifixion is on the reverse), the panel was part of a little folding altar.

Cologne, c. 1440

The Virgin Enthroned with the Infant Christ, Four Holy Virgins and Music-Making Angels

Panel, diameter: 85.8 cm – inv. no. WAF 500 – Acquired in 1827 from the Boisserée Collection

The Virgin is represented enthroned as the Queen of Heaven with SS Catherine, Barbara, Agnes and Apollonia. The way the anonymous painter has fitted the composition into the round is highly decorative. The schematic faces reveal that the painter learned his craft before Stefan Lochner reached the city on the Rhine. On the other hand, the angelic musicans attest to Lochner's influence on artists active in Cologne. The tondo came from the Cistercian Monastery of Mariaegarten in Cologne, which was disbanded in 1802.

Stefan Lochner

(Meersburg c. 1410 – Cologne 1451)

Outer panels of a hinged retable, c. 1440/50

Panel, 120 x 161 cm (overall) – inv. nos. WAF 501, WAF 502 – Acquired in 1827 from the Boisserée Collection

The following saints are represented on the two wings of the altarpiece: Antony Abbot (with bell), Pope Cornelius (with a horn, Latin cornu, alluding to his name), St Mary Magdalene (ointment jar), Catherine of Alexandria (sword and wheel), St Hubert (stag) and Quirin of Neuss (a banner with nine spheres alluding to Neuss, Latin: Novesium). In the foreground two unidentified donors are kneeling, depicted on a smaller scale than the saints as a sign of humility. Their armorial bearings are in the corners of the panels. The entire background was originally blue and the panels bore representations on both sides. On the front were representations of the

martyrdoms suffered by the twelve Apostles (Frankfurt). In the 19th century the panels, still in Cologne, were sawn into twelve pieces. Later the backs were detached and the array of saints was pieced together again. The panels were probably the wings of the altarpiece from St Laurence's church (Cologne) on which a Last Judgement was depicted because it bears the same donor coats of arms as the Munich panels.

As always, Lochner's figures are so light that they seem to hover above the ground. Plasticity is achieved mainly through the sophisticated play of light and shade rather than definition of corporeal mass. Some of the men look tired or sunk in thought. The women have round heads, small mouths and – hair was one of Lochner's specialities – fair hair. St Mary Magdalene has a speaking countenance: she looks saucy. The fabric of the figures' clothing subtly characterizes them and the softly falling folds are distinguished by beauty of line. Lochner seems here to be reverting to the style of the first quarter of the century. Meticulous attention to detail in the rendering of accessories and attributes attest to Lochner's Netherlandish training.

Gabriel Angler
(active between 1440 and 1460)

Crucifixion with SS Coloman, Quirin, Castor and Chrysogonus, c. 1440

Panel, 186 x 294 cm – inv. no. 1438 – Acquired in 1803 near Lake Tegernsee during secularization

A contemporary of Stefan Lochner's, Gabriel Angler was only identified a few years ago. He used to be called "The Master of the Tabula Magna" (large panel) from the high altar of the ancient Benedictine monastery church of St Quirinus, his masterpiece (now in Munich, Nuremberg and Berlin). The Crucifixion, with its depiction of Calvary, was a rood-screen made for the congregation of the church. Important saints flank the broad central scene: Coloman, an Irish pilgrim; Castor (left), a mason and martyr; Quirinus, a Roman Emperor's son; and the Roman teacher and martyr Chrysogonus, in scholar's robes (right). The church had preserved relics of three of these saints from the 8th and the 11th centuries. Veneration of St Coloman began in the 15th century after the Melk monastery reform had reached Tegernsee. The palette selected for the panel is unusual: the figures and the frame are skeuomorphically represented as if they were made of stone to fit in with their surroundings. The only accents of colour are the carnation (flesh tints), hair and metal elements. Although the area representing the ground is cut off in a rather archaic manner, Angler would not have been able to execute the foreshortened horses and the rear-view figure beneath the left-hand thief's cross without direct exposure to 14th-century northern Italian art. In fact, he is known to have gone to Venice to buy pigments.

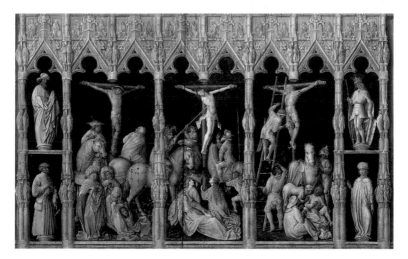

Master of the Polling Altar
(active c. 1440/50)

Panels of the Polling Altarpiece, c. 1440/50

Panel, each 219 x 87.5 cm – inv. nos. 1368, 1369 – Acquired from Polling in 1804 during secularization

A legend from the Bavarian Dark Ages: while stag hunting, Duke Tassilo II (reign 748-788) came across a doe which suddenly stopped, unafraid, and began to paw the ground with her hoofs. Three crosses came to light which were excavated under the supervision of a bish-op. Tassilo vowed to build a monastery to the glory of the Saviour and the Holy Cross on that very spot near Polling. Lavishly written and illustrated, the text of the legend was addressed to the Augustine canons and illiterate pilgrims who flocked to Polling to venerate the cross there. The legend "explained" the ducal foundation of the monastery as well as the origins of the "ancient" cross, which was displayed in a shrine closed off by the painted wings of this anonymous altarpiece. The cross is still in Polling and art historians date it to 1230.

Master of the Life of the Virgin
(active in Cologne c. 1460 – 1490)

The Birth of the Virgin, c. 1460/65
Panel, 85.6 x 109.5 cm – inv. no. WAF 619
– Acquired in 1827 from the Boisserée
Collection

The panel belongs to a cycle of
paintings although their actual
number is unknown (seven in
Munich and one in London). They
once hung in the church of St
Ursula in Cologne, either singly or
framed as a group. The Birth of the
Virgin is the most moving of these
paintings and is the work of a
mature painter. The anonymous
Cologne painter obviously learned
his craft during travels to the Netherlands and by studying similar
works in his native city (see Rogier
van der Weyden's St Columba
Altar). The sources of inspiration
drawn on by the painter are revealed
in details of the interior: furnishings, jugs, boxes, even the cushion

tossed carelessly on the floor in
front of the bed. Further, the genre
element is manifest in what is going
on in a typical room: the newborn
baby is being cared for, her bath is
being poured and her swaddling
clothes and a cloth are being made
ready. The baby's mother, Anne, is
being tenderly looked after. In German painting of this period, this
work is unique in its detail and naturalistic rendering of behaviour.
What seems to be a Cologne feature
is the delicacy of the figures. The
room, which begins with such a
convincing display of perspective in
the tiles, seems to end in a gold
background that does not really represent walls. Perhaps the man who
commissioned the painting, the
councilman and mayor Johann von
Hirtz (*d.* in 1481), wanted it this way
because he hoped that the precious
painting he had donated would look
extrinsically as well as intrinsically
valuable.

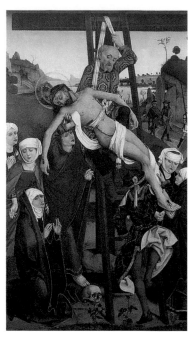

Hans Pleydenwurff

(Bamberg [?] c. 1420 –
Nuremberg 1472)

The Hof Altar, 1465

Panel, 178 x 451 cm (overall) – dated –
inv. nos. 663, 664, 666, 670 – Acquired
before 1816 as a present from the towns-
people of Hof to King Max I Joseph

In the Alte Pinakothek, Hans
Pleydenwurff represents the generation before Albrecht Dürer's
teachers. He left Bamberg for
Nuremberg, where he was made
a freeman of the Reich city in
1457. After his death, Michael
Wohlgemut married his widow
and took over his workshop,
where Albrecht Dürer slaved as a
pupil from 1486 after breaking
off his apprenticeship as a goldsmith in his father's workshop.
Pleydenwurff executed the hinged
altarpiece in 1465 for the high
altar of St Michael's Church in
Hof. The Crucifixion and the
Deposition are reproduced here,
the two central panels of four on
the back of the hinged retable
(not shown: Christ on the Mount
of Olives and the Resurrection).
The wings open out to reveal the
Annunciation and the Birth of
Christ as well as a gilt shrine with
carved figures. When the wings
are closed, the patron saint of the
church, the Archangel Michael,
with the Apostles Bartholomew
and James, is on view. Like the
Master of the Life of the Virgin,
Pleydenwurff was noticeably
influenced by Netherlandish
painting. Both artists assimilated
this inspiration to enrich what
they had acquired from their
native tradition, developing this
synthesis further to achieve
decidedly different results.

Michael Pacher

(Bruneck/Pustertal [?] c. 1435 –
Salzburg 1498)

The Martyrdom of St Laurence,
c. 1465/70

Panel, 102 x 99 cm – inv. no. 5306 –
Acquired in 1812 from the Augustine
chapter-house at Neustift near Brixen

Legend has it that Laurence, a
deacon, was roasted alive on a
grill. Even at the point of death,
he found the strength to mock his
torturers, requesting them to turn
him over so that he would brown
evenly on all sides. The panel
painting is one of the earliest
extant altarpieces of Pacher's, who
was both a sculptor and painter. It
was commissioned for the church
of St Laurence in Pustertal. While
the church was undergoing
Baroque renovation in the 17th
century, the retable was dis-
mantled. All that remained in situ
was the carved Madonna in the
shrine. When the wings of the
altarpiece were closed, four
scenes from the legend of St
Laurence were visible (inner face:
the Life of the Virgin). Michael
Pacher unites Late Gothic tradition with Renaissance innovation.
Direct contact with the work of
Mantegna is attested to by his
rendering of figures and handling
of perspective. The solutions he
found to these problems were to
remain a closed book to painters
north of the Alps for decades.

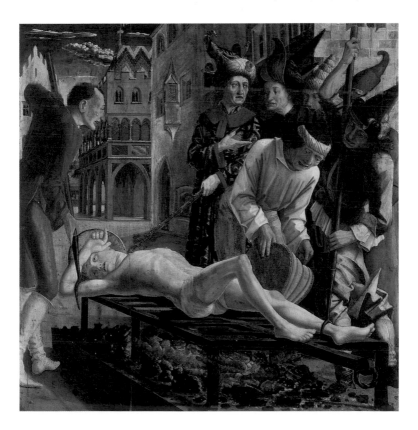

Michael Pacher

(Bruneck/Pustertal [?] c. 1435 – Salzburg 1498)

Altarpiece of the Four Latin Doctors, c. 1480

Panel, 216 x 380 cm (overall) – inv. nos. 2597-2600 – Acquired in 1812 during secularization from Neustift near Brixen

Once the high altar of the Augustine chapter church at Neustift near Brixen, this retable bears paintings on both sides and is without the carved shrine typical of Pacher's altarpieces. Nonetheless, as if he wanted to flaunt his other talent even here, Pacher has imitated in painting a shrine with sculpture, oddly enough not carved in wood but hewn from stone. The statement Pacher is making with such virtuosity is that painting can do anything. The four Latin Doctors of the Western Church are portrayed here. They are identified by the attributes legend links with them. Jerome is depicted drawing a thorn from the lion which served him in gratitude the rest of his life. Augustine is shown with the child who enlightened him metaphorically (by try-

ing to drain the sea dry with a spoon) on the impossibility of understanding the mystery of the Trinity. Pope Gregory the Great is depicted with the Emperor Trajan, whom he redeemed from Purgatory through prayer. Ambrose is represented with a child who cried out in a dispute between Arians and Catholics that Ambrose should be anointed bishop. The source on which all four Latin Doctors draw is divine inspiration in the form of the dove of the Holy Ghost. Pacher is at the height of his powers here. The narrow picture spaces beneath the flaring baldachins are drawn to scale with the tiles on the floor indicating perspective. The play of light from the right is dealt with consistently. However, what astounded art lovers in the 15th century and continues to do so in the 21st is the artist's handling of perspective in details: the lecterns, the cradle, Augustine's gesture of reaching out and, of course, the marvellous dove above his head. How odd that this work should mark the end of Pacher's activity in the Tyrol.

Martin Schongauer
(Colmar c. 1450 – Breisach 1491)

The Holy Family, c. 1475/80

Panel, 26 x 17 cm – inv. no. 1132 –
from the Zweibrücken Gallery

The representation takes up the
theme of the Flight into Egypt.
However, in the foreground, the
Virgin enthroned constitutes an
independent motif. She is giving
her child succory (chicory) as an
apotropaic measure.

Master of the Holy Kinship
*(active in Cologne late 15th/early 16th
century)*

St Antony Abbot as a Hermit,
c. 1500/10

Panel, 108.2 x 190.1 cm – inv. no. WAF 452
– Acquired in 1827 from the Boisserée
Collection

The unusual subject matter of this
panel painting is due to the loca-
tion for which it was commissioned, the church of the Order of
Hospitallers of St Antony in
Cologne, donated by Wenceslaus
Ulner, the preceptor of the order.
In the foreground a ninety-year-old
Antony is meeting Paul of Thebes,
the first hermit, at the spring in
front of the latter's cell. A raven
brings bread. The representations
in the background, left, treat of
events from Antony's life: Antony's
way into the desert, scenes of
temptation, the burial of Paul. On
the right posthumous events are
depicted, among them Antony's
body being conveyed from Egypt
by Bishop Theophilus. The panor-
amic format and high horizon
were inspired by Netherlandish art
(see Memling).

Master of St Bartholomew

(active in Cologne 4th quarter of the 15th/1st decade of the 16th century)

St Bartholomew Altar, c. 1500/05

Panel, 129 x 309 cm (overall) – inv. nos. 11863 11865 – Acquired in 1827 from the Boisserée Collection.

The panel reproduced here is the central one of a hinged retable which gave the anonymous painter his convenience name. SS Agnes, Bartholomew and Cecilia are depicted with a kneeling Carthusian monk. The wings (not shown here) bear representations of SS John the Evangelist, Margaret, James the Lesser and Christina. It has not been possible to clear up the question of where this altar was originally placed. In the upper corners the family marks and armorial bearings of Arnt von Westerburg and his wife, Druitgen von Andernach, are displayed. This would indicate

that the kneeling Carthusian was not the man who commissioned the panel. Still, both families were connected with the Carthusian monastery in Cologne. The Boisserées did not, however, acquire the altar from St Columba's Church. The anonymous painter, who probably trained in the Netherlands, was for decades a distinctive personality active in Cologne. His figures are invariably distinguished by great plasticity and gravity. He has a noticeable preference for certain types: women with round heads and small mouths and rather mournful-looking men. Iconographically unconventional and dramatic, the work of this highly skilled artist was obviously much in demand in Cologne. In the panel shown here, his mastery of landscape, often merely hinted at, is hidden by a curtain behind the figures.

Hans Holbein the Elder

(Augsburg c. 1465 – Upper Rhine 1524)

St Sebastian Altar, 1516

Panel, 153 x 200 cm (overall) – inv. nos. 669, 5352, 668 – Acquired in 1809 during secularization from the Jesuit church of St Salvator in Augsburg

Sebastian, captain of Praetorian Guards under the Emperor Diocletian, was a Christian who stood by martyrs till their deaths. When the emperor heard of this, he condemned Sebastian to death. Tied to a stake, he was shot at until he was so full of arrows "that he stood there like a hedgehog" (Legenda aurea). A few days later, the saint was seen standing in front of the imperial palace, miraculously cured of his wounds, to denounce the persecution of Christians. Sebastian was ultimately murdered and his corpse thrown into the Roman sewers, as shown in the background of the central panel. On the wings SS Barbara and Elizabeth are depicted (on the outer faces the Annunciation). These were the patron saints of those in danger of sudden death and those who prayed for a "gentle death". Sebastian's patronage was against the plague. Trusting in the saints he depicted, the devout artist represented himself as a bearded figure next to St Elizabeth. This High Renaissance retable is a mature work (compare the Kaisheim Altar, 1502, on the ground floor). The composition is built up around full-length figures viewed close up. The realism with which the foreground figures are depicted evokes immediacy. Ornament is in the antique style and the palette is light and heightened. Problems with representation of space – look at the contradictory relationship of the landscape, which crosses the bounds of the panels, to the Renaissance frame,

which looks as if it had been set in – are signs of the crisis which affected medieval church appointments at the end of an age.

Albrecht Dürer

(Nuremberg 1471 – Nuremberg 1528)

Portrait triptych of Oswolt Krel, 1499

Panel, 49.7 x 71 cm (overall) – inv. nos. WAF 230, 230a, 230b – Acquired in 1828 from the Oettingen-Wallerstein Collection

Between January 1499 and August 1500, Oswolt Krel was in Nuremberg as the chief accountant of the Great Ravensburg Merchant Society. During this time he had his portrait painted by Dürer. The piercing and critical glance which Dürer gave his sitter and the sitter's forceful grasp of his fur-trimmed cloak attest to the artist's intention of characterizing both the personality and the profession of the person portrayed. This is how one imagines a chief accountant of the period to have looked. Dürer chose a traditional type of portrait which he was able to market successfully more than once that same year. In all these portraits a curtain is the sitter's backdrop and at one side there is a narrow view into a landscape. The "Wild Men" on the side panels, which are mounted like a hinged altarpiece, clutch the Krel coat of arms (curving claws) and that of his wife, Agathe von Essendorf. The "Wild Men" were mythical figures, descendants of Cain as medieval legend has it. They hid in forest fastnesses, had shaggy fur and occasionally engaged knights in combat. Late Gothic art was particularly fond of this motif, which occurs in manuscript illumination, tapestries, carved in wood and as architectural sculpture in churches as well as in prints. The panels with the heraldic creatures have been mounted since 1911 as they are now. However, it is not known what function they originally served.

Albrecht Dürer
(Nuremberg 1471 – Nuremberg 1528)

Paumgartner Altar, c. 1500

Panel, c. 157 x 250 cm (overall) – mono-
grammed – inv. nos. 701, 706, 702 –
Acquired in 1613 by Duke Maximilian I of
Bavaria from St Catherine's Church in
Nuremberg

The central panel bears a representation of the Adoration of the infant
Christ by the Virgin, Joseph and
shepherds. The Paumgartner family and Barbara Paumgartner's second husband, Hans Schönbach, are
kneeling in worship in the foreground. On the wings appear SS
George and Eustachius as well as a
second representation of the brothers Stephan and Lukas Paumgartner. Dürer followed the Legenda
aurea in placing the Adoration of
the Christ Child by the Virgin in a
covered passage between two houses. The handling of the architecture reveals that Dürer was already
preoccupied with theories of perspective. The Paumgartner Altar
used to stand on the east wall of the
south side aisle of St Catherine's
in Nuremberg.

Albrecht Dürer
(Nuremberg 1471 – Nuremberg 1528)

**Self-Portrait in a Fur-Trimmed Coat,
1500**

Panel, 67.1 x 48.9 cm – signed and dated –
inv. no. 537 – Acquired in 1805 by the
Zentralgemäldegaleriedirektion

Dürer's self-portrait, completed in
1500, is remarkable in every way.
What is new to portraiture, still a
fledgling genre, is the severe fron-

tality of the sitter, recalling ideal representations of Christ. In the late Middle Ages exemplars of the "True Image of Christ" (vera icon) and half-length representations of the Saviour had a wide circulation. However, this Dürer self-portrait is just as closely linked with the theoretical studies of human proportions which Dürer was the first artist north of the Alps to engage in. The face and hands are emphasized to indicate that the chief tools of the artist's trade are his theme here: visual powers and creativity (the "hand" appears often in Dürer's theoretical writings as a metaphor for "art"). This is, in fact, a sophisticated programmatic representation of what art is all about. The Latin inscription in large letters reinforces the visual imagery: "Thus I, Albrecht Dürer of Nuremberg,

made an image of myself in appropriate colours in my 28th year."

Albrecht Dürer
(Nuremberg 1471 – Nuremberg 1528)

Glim Lamentation (Pietà), c. 1500

Panel, 151.9 x 121.6 cm – inv. no. 704 – Acquired between 1598 and 1607 by Duke Maximilian I of Bavaria

The Glim Lamentation is the funerary painting executed to commemorate the Nuremberg goldsmith Albrecht Glim and his wife, Margret Holtzmann. They are portrayed on a smaller scale with two sons and a daughter in the foreground. The composition is orientated to the left, perhaps due to where it was to be hung on a pillar in the Nuremberg Predigerkirche (Preacher's Church).

Albrecht Dürer
(Nuremberg 1471 – Nuremberg 1528)

Four Apostles, 1526

Panel, 213 x 152.5 cm (overall) – mono-
grammed and dated – inv. nos. 545, 540 –
Acquired in 1627 in Nuremberg by the
Prince Elector Maximilian I

Four slightly larger than life-size
figures are represented in the
narrow, unified picture space of
the two panels: John, Peter, Mark
and Paul. The narrow strip bearing the inscription at their feet is
incorporated in the picture plane.
The first sentence calls for "temporal princes" to revere the words
of the Bible and shun the bland-

ishments of "false prophets".
This "warning" is reinforced with
words from the writings ascribed
to the Apostles depicted. The
appearance of each saint and
their different personalities represent the spirit of the written word
in visual terms: irascible watch-
fulness and a menacing glare on
one side contrast with composed
contemplation of the words of the
Bible on the other. The masterpiece of Dürer's maturity, the
work is thematically linked with
the Reformation, which came to
Nuremberg in 1525. The artist
gave it to the Council of Burgess-
es of his native city.

Lucas Cranach the Elder
(Kronach 1472 – Weimar 1553)

The Death of Lucretia, 1524 (?)

Panel, 194 x 75 cm – Cranach signet – inv.
no. 691 – From the Kammergalerie of the
Prince Elector Maximilian I

The legend of Lucretia has a
temporal meaning with moral
overtones. Raped by Sextus Tar-
quin, son of the King of Rome,
Lucretia committed suicide. Her
act of courage in the face of dis-
honour marked the beginning of
the end of the Roman monarchy.

Lucas Cranach the Elder
(Kronach 1472 – Weimar 1553)

Crucifixion, 1503

Panel, 138 x 99 cm – dated – inv. no. 1416
– Acquired in 1804 during secularization

This Crucifixion is one of the earliest works extant from the hand of
Lucas Cranach the Elder. He probably painted it while on his travels
after a sojourn in Vienna and just
before he was appointed Painter to
the Court of Frederick the Wise of
Saxony. At thirty-one, the painter is
at the height of his powers in this
first large altarpiece. Although the
theme was traditionally represented on parallel planes, the Cross has
here been placed at an oblique
angle in the picture space like an
illustration of perspective theory.
The foreshortening of the figure of
the thief on the left edge of the picture plane is breathtakingly bold.
Counterbalancing the figure of the
Crucified and suffering his pain,
the Virgin is a focal point of the
composition.

Lucas Cranach the Elder
(Kronach 1472 – Weimar 1553)

The Golden Age, c. 1530

Panel, 73.5 x 105.5 cm – inv. no. 13175 –
Transferred from the state collections in
1961

Men and women are depicted
treading a tranquil measure round
a tree laden with fruit. This is the
earliest age of man without sorrow,
disease, old age, false modesty or
strife. Harmony and a pleasant,
relaxed way of life are the order of
the day. During the mythical Gold-
en Age, man and animal lived
peacefully together in a closed gar-
den. Ancient writings, rediscovered
in the Renaissance as material for
paintings, are the sources of this
utopia of the past. According to
Hesiod, the Golden Age was followed by the Silver Age and then
by the Bronze and Iron Ages.
However, the people who had lived
in the Golden Age lived on by the
will of Zeus as good spirits. It is
not known who commissioned the
panel.

Lucas Cranach the Elder
(Kronach 1472 – Weimar 1553)

**Cardinal Albrecht of Brandenburg
before Christ on the Cross, 1620s**

Panel, 158 x 112 cm – inv. no. 3819 –
Acquired in 1829 from the Aschaffenburg
Stiftskirche (collegiate church)

The man portrayed here had many
titles: Margrave of Brandenburg,
Archbishop of Magdeburg, Admin-
istrator of the Bishopric of Halber-

stadt, Archbishop and Prince Elector of Mainz and Cardinal. He was also a prominent patron of the arts. Cranach has portrayed him kneeling on a large cushion before the Crucified. This is not, however, your usual donor portrait nor does it represent a historical person being incorporated in a historic event. On the contrary, the Crucified is represented sketchily rather than realistically and is on a smaller scale than the figure of the Cardinal. The figure of Christ on the Cross is treated devotionally to represent the Passion as meditated on by the figure commemorated, the Cardinal. This is why he is portrayed looking off into the distance. Revealing Cranach's skill as a colourist, the portrait was based on a Dürer engraving. Contrasting sharply with their dark setting, the Cardinal's red vestments flatten out into an autonomous surface to create an astonishingly modern effect. This type of commemorative funerary portraiture was in use on into the 18th century.

Hans Burgkmair
(Augsburg 1473 – Augsburg 1531)

Altarpiece of St John on Patmos, 1518

Panel, 153 x 220 cm (overall) – signed and dated – inv. nos. 21, 685, 20 – From the Kammergalerie of Maximilian I

On this hinged altarpiece St John is depicted at the moment of revelation (the Apocalypse). St Erasmus is represented on the left and St Martin on the right. An imaginatively conceived tropical landscape extends across all three panels. Burgkmair may have gleaned his knowledge of tropical vegetation from prints or directly from the Fuggers' botanical gardens. The representations of the two Saints John on the outer faces of the panels have been detached. In the early 17th century the altarpiece was altered considerably. Pieces (covered by the frame) were added to the panels. The foliage at the top and some animals were covered and Erasmus' robes and the vision of the Virgin were repainted.

Albrecht Altdorfer ✓
(Regensburg [?] c. 1480 –
Regensburg 1538)

The Birth of the Virgin, c. 1520

Panel, 140.7 x 130 cm – inv. no. 5358 –
Acquired in 1816, probably from
Leopoldskron Castle, Salzburg

Altdorfer has moved this scene,
traditionally depicted in interiors in
any case, into the side aisle of a
church. A bed in the church would
not have bothered contemporary
viewers, who would have realized
that its presence there was
explained by the title of the altarpiece (St Anne Altar?). Viewed
obliquely, the problems posed by
architectural features of the interi-

or appear more complex than they
are. As an element of the composition, the large circle of dancing
angels wreathing the pier opens up
the picture space and defines it.
The cut-off figure of Joachim with
his purchases mediates between
the viewer and what is happening
in the picture space. The shell-like
apsidioles represent the newest
trend in Renaissance architecture
which Altdorfer could have studied
in Hans Hieber's model for the pil-
grimage church "of the Beautiful
Virgin" in his native Augsburg.
Conversely, Altdorfer was Town
Planner of Regensburg from 1526
so that he himself exerted an influence on architecture.

Albrecht Altdorfer

(Regensburg [?] c. 1480 – Regensburg 1538)

Susanna and the Elders, 1526

Panel, 74.8 x 61.2 cm – monogrammed and dated – inv. no. 698 – From the Ducal Kunstkammer in Munich, where it was recorded from 1598

Unlike later representations of the story, Altdorfer's does not show the moment Susanna, the lovely wife of a rich man named Joachim (Daniel 13), is surprised by the two Elders of Babylon. What you see here is both before and after the event. On the left the men are depicted lying under a tree lusting for the great moment. On the right, they are being stoned for calumny on the palace terrace. At the centre the young woman is innocently enjoying her bath, attended by her serving maids. The palace is a fantastic masterpiece, revealing the artist's imaginative grasp of representing architecture. Assimilating inspiration from Italian sources, Altdorfer was the first to use angular or two-point perspective in German art. A preliminary sketch is extant (Düsseldorf) with some deviation in details. It was apparently translated to the panel with the help of a quadratura, a perspective scheme.

Albrecht Altdorfer

(Regensburg [?] c. 1480 – Regensburg 1538)

The Battle of Issus, 1529

Panel, 158.4 x 120.3 cm – signed and dated – inv. no. 688 – From the Ducal Kunstkammer in Munich

The battle between Alexander the Great and the Persian King Darius III at Issus in 333 BC effectively stopped the Persian advance. Altdorfer shows the crucial turning point. Darius has turned to flee and Alexander is dashing after him. The painter's pictorial imagery transcends the narration of events: the moon of early morning and the setting sun represent the time framework of the battle. Encompassing the then known world, the sweeping bird's-eye view of the Mediterranean with Cyprus and Egypt indicates the historic scope of the event. Although the waves of moving masses are reflected in the turbulence of the clouds, the weather, just like the situation, is clearing. The work is part of a cycle of history paintings commissioned by Duke Wilhelm IV and Jacobaea of Baden.

Matthias Grünewald

(Würzburg [?] c. 1475/80 – 1528/31)

SS Erasmus and Maurice,
c. 1520/24

Panel, 226 x 176 cm – inv. no. 1044 –
Acquired in the early 19th century from the
Aschaffenburg collegiate church

In 1520 Albrecht of Brandenburg
had the Neues Stift in Halle furnished and appointed. Altars were
executed, some of them by the
Cranach workshop. In 1541, as the
Reformation advanced, Albrecht
had them brought to Aschaffenburg. Grünewald's panel stood on
the altar consecrated to Maurice,
the church's patron saint. His
meeting with St Erasmus as depicted here is not historical. The relationship between the two saints
can be read on a second level of
meaning. In 1516 Albrecht had
introduced the cult of Erasmus in
Halle. The saint is depicted here
as a portrait of Albrecht. Maurice,
whom the artist modelled on a
statue erected in the Stiftskirche
in 1520/21, was also the patron
saint of the Holy Roman Empire,
of which Albrecht was the most
powerful Prince Elector. Politics
and religion are inextricably inter-
twined in this work.

Hans Baldung Grien

(Schwäbisch-Gmünd 1484 or 1485 – Strasbourg 1545)

Nativity, 1520

Panel, 105.5 x 70.4 cm – monogrammed and dated – inv. no. 6280 – Acquired in 1814 from the Aschaffenburg Stiftskirche (collegiate church)

The wonder of the Nativity is set here in a ruined palace. Mary and Joseph are kneeling in adoration of the newborn Christ, who seems to radiate an unearthly glow. It illumines the entire room. Little angels are singing and the ox and ass witness the scene (Isaiah I, 3). In the background the doorless opening reveals the shepherds to whom the angel has just announced the joyous tidings. The Star of Bethlehem on the left is represented as a sun-like disc. The composition is unusual and difficult to approach in both senses of the word. A bulky, dark pillar obscures the view into the interior, forcing viewers to look for the Christ Child. Therein lies the deeper layer of meaning. Treating the subject as a night piece derives from Netherlandish painting and is found in Germany as early as Baldung's Freiburg Cathedral high altar. Like Grünewald's Erasmus and Maurice panel, Baldung's painting probably was among the original appointments of the Collegiate Church.

Hans Suess von Kulmbach
(Kulmbach c. 1480 – Nuremberg 1522)

Margrave Casimir of Brandenburg, 1511
Panel, 43 x 31.5 cm – monogrammed and dated – inv. no. 9482 – Acquired in 1928 on the art market

At thirty Margrave Casimir (1481–1527) had his portrait painted by Kulmbach, a pupil of Dürer's. He is portrayed wearing a wreath of carnations over the gold turban which, like the chain about his neck, bears an emblem, a candle snuffer. A pelican is embroidered on his jerkin. It is piercing its breast to feed its young on its blood (a well-known symbol for the sacrifice of Christ on the cross). On his cloak are crescent moons, representations of the winds and stars. This may have been a courtship portrait or perhaps the Margrave simply wanted to remind the Bavarian court of his existence. In 1504 he had been promised Susanna, the daughter of Albrecht IV, in marriage. He finally married her in 1518.

Hans Baldung Grien
(Schwäbisch-Gmünd 1484 or 1485 – Strasbourg 1545)

Philip the Warlike, Count Palatine, 1517
Panel, 41.5 x 30.8 cm – monogrammed and dated – inv. no. 683 – From Neuburg Castle on the Danube

Philip (1503–1548) was the younger brother of Ottheinrich, Count Palatine and later Prince Elector. Baldung has portrayed him as a young man, whose suspiciously shy glance does not disguise a forceful personality. He lived according to the motto: "Leave nothing untried" and this portrait convinces us that he did just that. Philip grew up in Neuburg. At the tender age of thirteen, he was elected rector of Freiburg University. Later he was to study in Italy. He probably received his nickname, "Bellicosus", for volunteering for service in the campaign against the Turks at the gates of Vienna (1529).

Hans Muelich (Mielich)
(Munich 1516 – Munich 1573)

Andreas Ligsalz and his wife Apollonia, née Ridler, 1540

Panel, each 81 x 61 cm – monogrammed and dated – inv. nos. 19, 12 – Acquired by the Prince Elector Karl Theodor in 1793

Andreas Ligsalz was a Munich patrician. He earned his fortune as a merchant and had a trading post in Antwerp. He also held political office in Munich: in 1523 he became a member of the Outer Council and, in 1526, of the Inner Council. He is also recorded as mayor. He and his wife, also from a Munich patrician family, lived in the house at 12 Hacken Strasse. In this diptych Muelich combines two different types of portrait: frontal and not quite half profile. The pose taken by Ligsalz's wife lends the whole a touch of spontaneity and liveliness.

Italian Painting from the 14th to the 16th Century

Italian altarpieces are quite different from those found in churches north of the Alps. The Italians were not interested in opening and changing an altarpiece to suit the Church calendar. Instead, the Italian retable was more like a permanent devotional image. The main subject matter, with representations from the Life of Christ and the lives of the saints, is the Virgin, with the infant Christ or the Holy Family, suffering or glorified. Profane and mythological subject matter for collectors and humanist connoisseurs is encountered in Italy much earlier than north of the Alps. Portraits of individuals also became widespread in Italy during the 15th century. Florence and Venice are superbly represented in the Alte Pinakothek with paintings by Fra Angelico, Botticelli, Perugino, Leonardo, Raphael, Titian and Tintoretto. Most of these were acquired in the early 19th century by Crown Prince Ludwig, who became King Ludwig I of Bavaria.

Giotto di Bondone
(Colle di Vespignano ca. 1267 – Florence 1337)

The Last Supper, c. 1306
Panel, 42.5 x 43 cm – inv. no. 643 – Presented by Crown Prince Ludwig in 1805

Giotto is regarded as the founder of modern painting because he confronted the formulaic, Byzantine-influenced "maniera greca" of the 13th century with new challenges. The emphatic plasticity of his figures is articulated by the voluminous shapes of their robes and large heads. Facial expression and gestures are lively in Giotto. Interiors, as here, often resemble the box-like medieval stage. Coffered ceilings and multiple overlayering of the figures define space. The earliest assured Giottos are in Assisi but much has been lost (Rome, Naples). The *Last Supper* was part of an altarpiece which was probably executed in his workshop soon after the frescoes in the Arena Chapel in Padua.

Taddeo Gaddi
(Florence c. 1300 – Florence 1366)

St Francis' Trial by Fire, c. 1340
Panel, 34.6 x 31.3 cm – inv. no. 10677 – Acquired in 1940 from a private collection

In the presence of the Sultan of Egypt, St Francis of Assisi offered to submit to walking through fire to demonstrate the power of the Christian faith. Fearing a popular rebellion, the Sultan would not let his imams emulate St Francis. With 27 other paintings, this panel by Giotto's pupil decorated a sacristy cupboard in Santa Croce, Florence.

Lippo Memmi
(recorded 1317 – 1347)

The Assumption, c. 1340
Panel, 72.5 x 32.5 cm, in the original frame – inv. no. WAF 671 – Acquired before 1825 by Crown Prince Ludwig

Music-making angels accompany the Virgin to Heaven. Christ and the prophets of his coming await her in the starry vault of Heaven. In the peak of the gable is a representation of the Coronation of the Virgin. The Sienese painter Lippo Memmi was the brother-in-law of Simone Martini, a pupil of Duccio's. Memmi did not rely on tradition for this painting. Since the thematic content was recent, he was free to invent an original iconographic solution, which was often copied.

Masolino da Panicale
(Panicale c. 1383 – Florence c. 1447)

Virgin and Child, c. 1435
Panel, 95.5 x 57 cm – inv. no. WAF 264 – Acquired by King Ludwig I after 1826

Masolino represents the International Gothic style, popular in Europe during the first quarter of the 15th century. Its salient characteristic is softly flowing folds depending more on beauty of line than realistic rendering of the properties of fabric. Even after collaborating with Masaccio on the Brancacci Chapel, Masolino remained true to this style. The well-known motif of the Madonna with bared breast ("del latte") is combined here with the Madonna of humility ("dell'umiltà). Half enthroned, the Virgin is also kneeling. God the Father and the dove of the Holy Ghost expand the iconography into a representation of the Holy Trinity.

Fra Angelico
(Vicchio 1386/1400 – Rome 1455)

The Entombment, c. 1438/40

Panel, 37.9 x 46.4 cm – inv. no. WAF 38a –
Acquired in 1818 for the collection owned
by Crown Prince Ludwig

Joseph of Arimathaea is supporting
the lifeless but nearly erect body of
Christ before the open mouth of
the tomb. The Virgin and St John
devoutly take the hands of the
Redeemer and kiss them. No one
touches him directly. They are
depicted as being so in awe of him
that they use cloths to do so. There
is no voiced lamentation. All is
silent veneration. The Dominican
father Fra Angelico has obviously
not narrated a consistent scene
here. What does occur is limited
and not logically coherent. The artist's representation leaves hapless
art historians groping for the right
words. The panel was once the centre of the predella of the high altar

in San Marco, Florence. In front of
it, the Transubstantiation celebrat-
ing the sacrifice of the Redeemer
took place on the altar table. The
painting evokes the liturgical act of
the priest who raises aloft the consecrated wafer before laying it on
the corporal. The posture of Christ
in the painting alludes to the Crucifixion, the Deposition and the old
icon of the imago pietatis. The
open mouth of the tomb bears the
same relationship to the body of
Christ as the tabernacle does to the
consecrated host. The motif is as
memorably mnemonic as a picto-
graph. Three other predella panels
show the legend of the martyred
brothers and doctors Cosmas and
Damian, patron saints of the city of
Florence and the House of Medici,
who endowed the Sylvestrine monastery with appointments and furnishings. The central panel of the
altarpiece is in the Museo San Marco, Florence.

Fra Filippo Lippi

(Florence c. 1406 – Spoleto 1469)

The Annunciation, c. 1450

Panel, 203 x 186 cm – inv. no. 1072 –
Acquired for the Bavarian royal collection
from the Suore Murate Convent, Florence,
in the early 19th century

The Virgin stands to receive
Gabriel's greeting but does not
see God the Father, accompanied
by Cherubim, and the dove of
the Holy Ghost. However, as if
aware of their presence, she
humbly casts down her eyes and
lays her hands on her breast,
submissively indicating her
answer. This delicate figure, rapt
in thought, is still fully Gothic in
mood. What is Renaissance, on
the other hand, is the largely decorative deployment of motifs. A
view into a doubly enclosed gar-
den through the central arch can
be interpreted as a reference to
the "murate" (immured) in the
manner of a speaking coat of
arms or impresa but, at the same
time, and perhaps causally
linked to it, also to the motif of
the "hortus conclusus", the "gar-
den inclosed" of the Song of Solomon (4, 12). Like the lily carried
by the angel, it is a symbol of vir-
ginity and the Immaculate Conception.

Antonello da Messina
(Messina c. 1430 – Messina 1479)

**The Virgin of the Annunciation,
c. 1473/74**

Panel, 42.5 x 32.8 cm – inv. no. 8054 –
Acquired in 1897

The Virgin of the Annunciation
without angels is a motif often
encountered as late as the 18th
century. Antonello's is a superb
rendering of it, notable for profound empathy with the youthful,
even child-like girl, who is
astounded yet submissive to God's
will. In Italian the term "annunzia-
ta" sums up this abbreviated type
of representation of the Annunciation. Much of the charm of this
work lies in the contrast between a
dark background, the Virgin's brilliant blue gown and the modelling
play of light and shade on her face
and hands. The books on the bal-
ustrade are arranged as a still life,
a pictorial device known to Antonello from Netherlandish painting,
which also inspired him, as a
young painter, to work in oils.

Leonardo da Vinci
(Vinci 1452 – Cloux near Amboise 1519)

Virgin and Child, c. 1473

Panel, 62 x 47.5 cm – inv. no. 7779 –
Acquired from a private collection in 1889

Here the universal genius – architect, sculptor, engineer and scholar
– reveals himself as still a young
painter in Verrocchio's workshop.
Nonetheless, this early work already
attests to his independence and
powers of invention. The Madonna
and Child are placed in a hall at a
parapet. In the background, win-
dows open to a mountain landscape
in the middle distance. The fluid
handling of this delicate rendition
of the Virgin, the subtly modulating
play of light throughout and the
airy landscape in which he has captured the very breezes anticipate
the artist's mature work. The brilliant experimenter and master of
technique seems to bow to mechan-
ical difficulties. Surface wrinkles,
noticeably in the rendering of the
Virgin's face, indicate the use here
of an unstable vehicle to bind the
pigments.

Sandro Botticelli

(Florence 1445 – Florence 1510)

Lamentation (Pietà), c. 1490

Panel, 140 x 207 cm – inv. no. 1075 –
Acquired for Crown Prince Ludwig in 1814

Botticelli epitomizes to many the ideal of the Renaissance painter, the creator of lovely Madonnas and masterpieces of pagan mythology for the Medici. Here, however, influenced by the Dominican preacher Savonarola, Botticelli seems to have forgotten his past. No longer content with painting beauty, he is not striving for a beautiful style. Eschewing spatial depth and landscape, he has instead concentrated ruthlessly on the brutality of the scene before the yawning entrance to the tomb. Drastically subordinating the figures to the thematic content, he has forced them into the constraints of a markedly symmetrical choreography. Dystopian criticism of the present is notably often forced to seek shelter in a "better" past. That may be why this composition seems to represent a reversion to the "maniera greca" of the 13th century. The Lamentation interpolated into the Bible story has always offered a multi-layered referential framework. At the centre of this "Vesper picture" stands the maternal Virgin. The pale incarnation of the swooning figure corresponds to that of the dead Christ. Treatises on the Passion relate that the Virgin's compassionate sorrow was so intense that she wanted to die with her son. Extreme mariolatry has even credited her with a share in humanity's Redemption. The gesture of the figure partly hiding her face, clutching the nails still covered in blood, is directed as much at the viewer as at the mute mourners. An appeal to meditation on the Passion, the work also invites thought on the "instruments of torture". Saints Jerome, Paul and Peter were added to the scene because the altarpiece was originally commissioned for the Pauline monastery in Florence.

Pietro Perugino
*(Città della Pieve 1445 – Fontignano,
near Perugia 1523)*

The Vision of St Bernard of Clairvaux,
c. 1490/94

Panel, 173 x 170 cm – inv. no. WAF 764 –
Acquired for King Ludwig I from the House
of Capponi, Florence, in 1829/30

The Virgin appeared to the mystic
and theologian when he was writ-
ing theological treatises, providing him with "first-hand" information. Called "doctrina", this
type of representation is associated with the iconography of the
saint. Perugino has represented
the scene in an open hall with
several aisles, which affords a
view of gently rolling hills. The
stylized landscape with its attenuated, fragile-looking trees, and the
oval heads, pointed mouths and
rosy incarnation of the figures are
typical of Perugino. These features also recur in the early work
of his celebrated pupil, Raphael.
However, under the influence of
Fra Bartolommeo, Leonardo and
Michelangelo, Raphael's work
developed rapidly in a different
direction. At the time of Raphael's
death, his teacher, on the other
hand, was still faithful to the style
which had always been so successful. The altarpiece shown
here came from the Nasi family
chapel in Santa Maria Maddalena
dei Pazzi in Florence.

Domenico Ghirlandaio

(Florence 1449 – Florence 1494)

The Virgin with the Infant Christ and SS Dominic, Michael, John the Baptist and John the Evangelist, c. 1494

Panel, 221 x 198 cm – inv. no. 1078 – Acquired by Crown Prince Ludwig from the House of Medici in 1816

This is the central panel of the high altar of the Dominican church of Santa Maria Novella in Florence. Ghirlandaio also decorated the church chancel with a masterly fresco. The altarpiece comprises two wings with representations of SS Laurence and Catherine of Siena. Deriving from Revelation (12,1-2: "a woman clothed with the sunne"), the Madonna in a Glory also symbolizes the Immaculate Conception, the maternity of the Virgin and the Assumption. The motif reflects in the tradition of hieratic, dogma-linked medieval representations of the Virgin. By contrast, the figures below the Virgin have local associations as the founder of the order (St Dominic) and the patron saints of the city (Michael and John the Baptist). The donor of the altarpiece was Giovanni Tornabuoni, represented by John the Evangelist, his patron saint. There could be no sharper contrast than that between the plasticity and clarity of contour distinguishing these figures and the Umbrian painting next to it.

Luca Signorelli

(Cortona c. 1445 – Cortona 1523)

Virgin and Child, 1495/98

Panel, diameter 87 cm, in the original
frame – inv. no. 7931 – Acquired in
Florence in 1894

A circular support, the tondo presents artists with a great challenge to their powers of inventiveness in composition. Derived from ancient art and heightening the subject matter thus displayed, the tondo was often used in the quattrocento for representations of the Virgin. The main problem with using it is making the composition plausible. As a rule, standing figures are not (or only rarely) used. Most are seated or half-length so that they can be fitted into the round without losing the monumentality expressive of heightening. The centre of Signorelli's tondo is dominated by a weighty Madonna. The gesture of adoration with which she turns to the tiny Christ Child, leaning in a relaxed pose at her knee, entails complex movement. In the background, right, a naked figure is seated, removing his sandals. A type assimilated from the Hellenistic-Roman "Thorn Picker", his iconographic significance here has not been satisfactorily explained. He obviously does act as a counterpoise in the composition. Signorelli's influence is still felt in Michelangelo's work.

Cima da Conegliano
(Conegliano c. 1460 –
Conegliano 1517/18)

Virgin and Child with SS Mary Magdalene and Jerome, c. 1496

Panel, 79.6 x 122.9 cm – signed – inv. no. 992 – Acquired in 1815 from the collection of the Empress Josephine in Malmaison

The "sacra conversazione" between the Madonna and saints developed from the 13th century in full-length or half-length figure representations. The latter were particularly popular in 15th-century Venice. Cima's Virgin Enthroned has turned to Jerome, who is represented as a penitent, without looking at him. By contrast, the infant Christ and Mary Magdalene, also iconographically established as a penitent, are looking directly at each other. The Child's purposeful gesture of reaching for the ointment jar prefigures for both his death on the Cross.

Jacopo de' Barbari
(Venice – The Netherlands before 1516)

Still Life with Partridge, Steel Gauntlets and Cross-Bow Bolts, c. 1504

Panel, 52 x 42.5 cm – signed and dated – inv. no. 5066 – From Neuburg Castle on the Danube

This still life is the earliest example of its type. Consummate trompe l'oeil evokes the objects hanging on the wall together with the cartellino bearing the painter's name. A Venetian, he was active at several European courts.

Lorenzo Lotto
(Venice c. 1480 – Loreto 1556)

The Mystic Marriage of St Catherine of Alexandria, c. 1505/08

Panel, 71.3 x 91.2 cm – signed – inv. no. 32 – Acquired in 1804 from the Prince-Bishop's Palace, Würzburg

Raphael
(Urbino 1483 – Rome 1520)

The Canigiani Holy Family, c. 1505/06

Panel, 131 x 107 cm – signed – inv. no. 476 – Given to Johann Wilhelm of the Palatinate by Grand Duke Cosimo III of Tuscany in 1691

Lorenzo Lotto is an idiosyncratic figure. Although he began by borrowing heavily from Giovanni Bellini, he soon blended Mannerist elements in his work: flickering reflected light, obscure spatiality and exalted gestures. As popular legend has it, Catherine of Alexandria was a noblewoman who sought a husband more noble, handsome, wise and rich than she was. A hermit suggested Christ as the answer. Catherine is depicted as seeing him in a dream after her baptism, when he puts a ring on her finger, symbolizing the *unio mystica*.

Raphael presents his Holy Family in a tectonic composition. All figures are subordinated to the stringently pyramidal scheme. Intimacy is reserved for the internal arrangement of axes and relationships developed among the figures and tied tightly into the composition. The artist's accurate observation of human behaviour makes the picture look natural despite the stringency of composition imposed on it. The groups of angels, so important as a counterpoise to the central composition, were painted over in the 18th century and not exposed to view again until 1983.

Raphael

(Urbino 1483 – Rome 1520)

Madonna della Tenda, c. 1513/14

Panel, 65.8 x 51.2 cm – inv. no. WAF 797 –
Acquired by Crown Prince Ludwig in 1819

The "Madonna with a Curtain"
marks a sudden new departure
in Raphael's work after he
moved to Rome. Unlike the figures in the Florentine Holy Family, these have become substantially more three-dimensional
and massive. The composition is
related to the "Mass at Bolsena"
(1512) in the Stanza d'Eliodoro,
finished shortly before this piece.
There are also echoes of
Michelangelo's sculpture (Tondo
Taddei, Pitti) and, significantly,

of figures in the lunette and win-
dow arch frescoes of the Sistine
Chapel.

Piero di Cosimo
(Florence c. 1462 – Florence 1521)

The Myth of Prometheus, c. 1515/20
Panel, 66 x 118.7 cm – inv. no. 8973 –
acquired from a private collection in 1918

Not all the scenes can be interpreted here. At the centre is the
statue fashioned from clay and
on the right Minerva is advising
Prometheus to quicken him into
life with the touch of a torch. In
the background she is flying up
into the sky with him so that he
can steal fire from the sun. On
the right a troglodyte dwells
beneath a cliff, a prehistoric den-
izen of earth. What is represented on the left is probably the
similar but failed attempt at
creating life made by Epimetheus, Prometheus' brother. Zeus
punished Epimetheus by trans-
forming him into a monkey. The
robed figure may be the father
of the gods, whose handiwork is
being admired by a kneeling Epimetheus. The panel was part of a
painted chest (cassone). There
is a companion piece in Strasbourg.

Titian
*(Pieve di Cadore c. 1487/90 –
Venice 1576)*

Vanity, c. 1515
Canvas, 97 x 81.2 cm – inv. no. 483 – From
the Kammergalerie of the Prince Elector
Maximilian I

This is an early Titian. Comparison
with the works reproduced on the
following pages clearly illustrates
the development that the artist
would go through in his long
career. The allegorical personifica-
tion of Vanity later underwent
modification, probably by Titian

himself, in some respects. Originally devoid of reflection, the looking-glass may contain jewels and coins as well as a crone with a distaff. The lady herself may hold an extinguished candle. All these changes enhanced the aspect of the transience of earthly things.

iconographic rarity. Her presence here is perhaps due to a personal wish expressed by the man who commissioned the work. The small format, too, would suggest use in private devotions. Large altarpieces are rare in Palma's work.

Jacopo Palma il Vecchio
(Serina near Bergamo c. 1480 – Venice 1528)

Titian
(Pieve di Cadore c. 1487/90 – Venice 1576)

Virgin and Child with SS Roch and Aurea, c. 1515

Panel, 67.6 x 92.6 cm – inv. no. 505 – From the Düsseldorf Gallery

Madonna and Child in an Evening Landscape, c. 1560

Canvas, 173.5 x 132.7 cm – signed (spurious signature?) – inv. no. 464 – Acquired in 1814 in Paris for King Max I

Starting where the early Titian left off, Palma is notable for his voluptuous handling of figures. Here SS Roch and Aurea are approaching the infant Christ on their knees. Seated on the Virgin's lap, the Christ Child hands a rosary to Roch. The Early Christian martyr Aurea is an

The Virgin is gazing in wonder and pride at the lively child on her lap whom she can only restrain somewhat by keeping a firm hold of his foot. Looking remarkably grown up for this motif, the Christ Child is not the cuddly newborn baby you might

expect. Titian may have wanted to prefigure the Herculean task awaiting him: the Redemption of humanity. In fact, he recalls representations of the infant Hercules. The right half of the representation is a view of an evening landscape, equally distinguished by the atmospheric quality evoked by the treatment of light and the unrestrained handling of the figure group.

Titian

(Pieve di Cadore c. 1478/90 – Venice 1576)

Christ Crowned with Thorns, c. 1570

Canvas, 280 x 182 cm – inv. no. 2272 – Recorded in 1748 in Schleissheim

This painting represents the zenith of Titian's late work and is one of the most celebrated in the Alte Pinakothek. Christ has seldom been portrayed as such a lonely figure yet here he is enmeshed in the toils of his torturers, who are pressing the Crown of Thorns down on his head with long poles. Even more figures crowd in from the right, jostling their way up the steps to mock him. The handling of the whole scene is characteristic of the late Titian: objects dissolve in masses of colour. The eerily flickering light from the suspended chandelier is caught up in moving reflections echoing the agitated brushwork. This is a turbulent picture. Only when viewed at a distance does the picture surface fuse into a picture plane to reveal recognisable objects and figures. The composition, too, is masterly. The discrepancy in weight between left and right enhances its dynamics. The long poles knit the complex figure group into a whole. In a version painted twenty-five years before this one (Paris, Louvre), Titian depicted Christ groaning in pain. In the Munich version Christ endures his fate stoically. Perhaps this change in attitude reflects the personal situation of the elderly artist, who has grown wise and patient with the years.

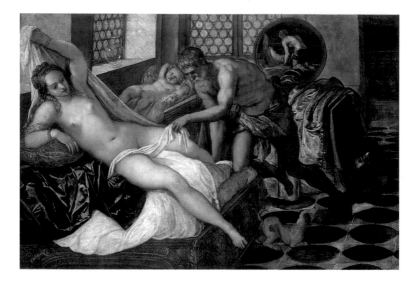

Jacopo Tintoretto
(Venice 1518 – Venice 1594)

**Vulcan Surprising Venus and Mars,
c. 1555**

Canvas, 135 x 198 cm – inv. no. 9257 –
Acquired in 1925 from the F.A. Kaulbach
estate

The story of Venus' adultery is
known from the Odyssey and
Ovid's Metamorphoses. Here
moralizing components have been
added. Vulcan suspiciously
inspects his wife's bed. Fully
accoutred, the god of war hides
under the table, where he vainly
attempts to stop the lady's lap-dog
from yapping. Ancient mythology
with a robustly humorous touch
yet the representation has yet to be
exhaustively interpreted. The som-
nolent Cupid is after a Venetian
copy of an ancient work. Emphasis
on interior perspective and exag-
geratedly lengthened figures are
typical of Jacopo Tintoretto, representing the Mannerist elements he
introduced to Venetian art.

Jacopo Tintoretto
(Venice 1518 – Venice 1594)

**The Capture of Parma,
c. 1579/80**

Canvas, 212 x 283.5 cm – inv. no. 7306 –
Recorded in Schleissheim in 1748

The scene is part of the Gonzaga
Cycle of history paintings. Two
series of four scenes each narrate
major events in the lives of the
15th-century margraves and 16th-
century dukes of Gonzaga.
Guglielmo Gonzaga, third Duke
of Mantua, commissioned the
cycle to commemorate the deeds
of his famous ancestors and had
it hung in two halls of the Palazzo Ducale at a height of 5 metres
off the floor. The last Gonzaga
took it with him into exile. It was
bequeathed to Duke Leopold of
Lorraine, who evidently sold it.
The scene shown here is the capture of Parma by Federico II, who
reconquered the city, occupied
by French troops, in 1521 for the
Vatican State.

Jacopo Tintoretto

(Venice 1518 – Venice 1594)

Christ with Mary and Martha, c. 1580

Canvas, 200 x 132 cm – signed – inv. no.
4788 – Acquired from the Dominican
church in Augsburg in 1803 during
secularization

The representation draws on
Luke 10, 38–42 and was executed
at the same time as Tintoretto's
paintings for the Scuola di San
Rocco. Christ has been invited to
the house of the sisters Mary and
Martha of Bethany. Martha is the
hostess and complains that she is
left with all the housework while
her sister Mary is listening to the
words of Christ. Christ replies
that Mary "hath chosen the good
part". The Bible story is often
quoted as an example of the "vita
activa et contemplativa", an inte-
gral part of both ancient and
medieval ethics. Tintoretto nar-
rates several parts of the story
simultaneously. In the background, right, Martha is working.
Viewed through the open door

and sketchily indicated, the disciples who accompanied Christ
everywhere are visible on the left.
While Christ is still talking to
Mary, Martha is already complain-
ing. The painting was probably
commissioned by the Welsers for
an altar in the Dominican church
in Augsburg.

Giorgio Vasari

(Arezzo 1511 – Florence 1574)

The Holy Family with the Young St John, c. 1545

Panel, 96 x 73 cm – inv. no. WAF 1150 – Acquired by Crown Prince Ludwig before 1810

Painter, architect and chronicler of art and artists, Giorgio Vasari was a typically versatile man of the Renaissance. His activities in Florence included building the Uffizi and painting the frescoes in the Palazzo Vecchio. His *Lives of the Artists*, published in several books in 1550 and 1568, still belong to art historians' tools of the trade. Vasari is indeed deservedly styled the Father of Art History. Decidedly retrospective and eclectic, Vasari's painting drew on the work of Michelangelo and Raphael. However, it is also Mannerist in implying that art could go no further in imitating nature and should therefore become artificial again. His aesthetic is grounded on affected flatness, smoothness of line and movement and figures cut off by the edge of the picture plane. His colour is broken, applied as an optical mixture and not blended before use. Every square centimetre of Vasari's work is art for art's sake.

Painting between Renaissance and Baroque

The 16th century cannot be
classified under a period
heading. "Mannerism" is
merely one of many phe-
nomena to emerge in this
multifaceted century. In this
section German and Netherlandish paintings are hung
side by side. The work of the
elder Pieter Brueghel launch-
es a new world view, combi-
ning humorous pictorial
anecdotes drawn from liter-
ature with a moral message.
His son, Jan Brueghel (nick-
named "Velvet" Brueghel for
his elegant handling of
fabric and flower textures),
built on his father's work.
The Alte Pinakothek, with
Vienna and Madrid, boasts
the world's largest Jan Brueghel collection. He is a contemporary both of Peter Paul
Rubens and the idiosyncratic
Adam Elsheimer, who set
new standards in nocturnal
landscape painting. The
Courtly Mannerism culti-
vated by artists working for
the Emperor Rudolf II in
Prague is represented here
by Spranger, von Aachen
and Heintz.

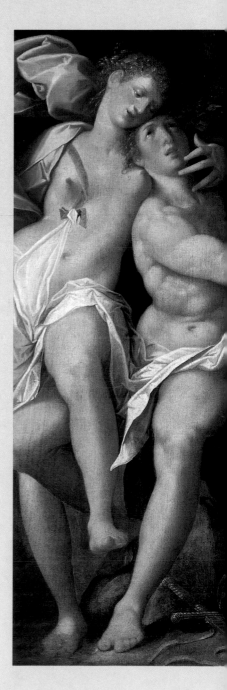

Jan Sanders van Hemessen
(Hemixen c. 1504 – Haarlem before 1567)

The Calling of Matthew, 1536
Panel, 118.8 x 153.9 cm – signed and dated – inv. no. 11 – From the Kammergalerie of the Prince Elector Maximilian I

This painting was originally one of those representations of a money-changer's office which were so popular in the Netherlands in the early 16th century. They reflect the reality of a greedy society but also often constitute a moral appeal for rejection of vices like avarice and greed. During the reign of the Prince Elector Maximilian I, the painting was worked over between 1627 and 1641. It was widened on the right and the top and the figure of Christ was presumably added by the court painter, Georg Vischer. Christ is summoning, underscored by the inscription: "Sequere me" ("Follow me": Mat. 9, 9). An iconographic novelty with a relevant message was thus launched. The calling of the Apostle was often represented during the 16th and 17th centuries. The associated theme of "God's grace" was raised to doctrinal significance by the Tridentine Council. The Church insisted on the importance of the person whom God's grace touches having free will. That is shown here. Levi, a customs official, was free to choose a different way of life and followed Christ voluntarily as Matthew when the call came. Considering the importance of the subject matter at the time, the radical intervention in the support and, more importantly, thematic content of the painting seems surprisingly logical on the metaphorical plane. Christ made a disciple of a customs official. The Prince Elector had a representation of sinful behaviour converted – missionary activity of a different kind.

Pieter Bruegel (Brueghel)
(Breda c. 1525 – Brussels 1569)

The Land of Cockayne, 1566
Panel, 52 x 78 cm – signed and dated – inv. no. 8940 – Acquired in 1917, once in the imperial collection, Prague

Paradise? The literary source is a tale published in 1546 in Antwerp after an anecdote about Hans Sachs which censures idleness, gluttony and sloth.

Cornelis van Dalem
(Antwerp? c. 1530/35 – Breda 1573)

Landscape with Farmstead, 1564
Panel, 103 x 127.5 cm – monogrammed and dated – inv. no. 12044 – Acquired from a private collection in 1954

An unusual example of what was then still a fledgling genre. Landscape as a vehicle for conveying mood. The charm of decay would not be appreciated again until the Romantic period.

Jan Brueghel

(Brussels 1568 – Antwerp 1625)

Port with Christ Preaching to the Multitude, 1598

Panel, 78 x 119 cm – signed and dated –
inv. no. 187 – From the Mannheim Gallery

A vast crowd of people is depicted. Clothing glows in touches of yellow, blue, red and green. Clearly demarcated into three planes of uniform tonality – brown in the foreground, green in the middle distance and blue in the background – the ground intervenes to articulate the picture surface. The planes direct the viewer's eye across the "earthly landscape", which conforms to 16th-century taste in the geographical and geological formation of the earth and is, of course, anything but realistic. The clear division of planes corresponds to a separation of levels of content. In the middle distance the crowd is intent on Christ, who is preaching from a boat on the Lake of Gennesaret (Luke 5, 3). The foreground, however, is filled with the hubbub of a fish market and is directed at the viewer. Dressed more for a Sunday stroll than workday shopping, elegant figures also walk about here among the fishmongers, whose wares are displayed like still lifes. Beggars are rewarded with an occasional coin as well as fish offal. All these figures look as if they were posing for the painter. Even more scenes from everyday life frame the market to distract viewers and keep their eyes roving. The religious theme has been pushed aside, not for lack of respect, but simply to integrate it into the mundane affairs of everyday living. The Alte Pinakothek possesses several such works by Jan Brueghel in which the artist has embellished ideal landscape types with details that are "naer het leven" ("close to life").

Jan Brueghel
(Brussels 1568 – Antwerp 1625)

Large Fishmarket, 1603

Panel, 58.5 x 91.5 cm – signed and dated – inv. no. 1889 – From the Mannheim Gallery

Here, as in the work hung next to it, the artist has incorporated as much real life as possible into the picture from his lofty vantage point. In this painting, however, the hustle and bustle of a port is his principal subject matter. There is no reference to religious content. Like the perspective from which the scene is viewed, the city, too, is ideal. It is a composite of Flemish architecture and impressions of landmarks the artist sketched while in Italy between 1590 and 1596. In the middle distance, for instance, you spot the Neapolitan Castel dell'Ovo and on the right St Peter's in Rome. Castel dell'Ovo crops up again in *The Continence of Scipio*.

Jan Brueghel
(Brussels 1568 – Antwerp 1625)
Pieter van Avont (?)
(Mechelen 1600 – Deurne 1652)

Holy Family, c. 1620

Panel, 93.5 x 72 cm – inv. no. 149 – From the Kurfürstliche Galerie (Prince Elector's Gallery)

The figures in this painting are the work of Pieter van Avont. The garland forms an M (for Mary).

Abraham Bloemaert
(Gorinchem 1566 – Utrecht 1651)

The Marriage of Peleus and Thetis, c. 1595

Canvas, 101 x 146.4 cm – inv. no. 6526 –
From the Kurmainzische Galerie
Aschaffenburg

All the Olympian gods were invited to the marriage of Peleus and Thetis. Only Eris (Strife), sister of Mars, god of war, was forgotten. She took sophisticated revenge by casting a gold ball inscribed with "for the most beautiful" into the crowd to stir up strife among the female guests. She was highly successful. The judgement of Paris which followed on the beauty contest between Hera, Athena and Aphrodite ultimately led to the Trojan war. A swirl of figures, fabric and clouds wrenches the viewer's gaze into an unreal picture space. The revolving figures in affected poses, carrying out meaningless actions and inter-locked in complex groupings, have been drastically subordinated to an ornamental conception of composition. The artist has eschewed the naturalistic approach in all respects. The composition flickers and shimmers to distract the eye. This a Mannerist collector's item of the type particularly popular at the Prague imperial court. Thematic content has become so unimportant that it is arbitrary. The composition goes back to an engraving, popular at the time, after a representation of the Marriage of Eros and Psyche (Hendrick Goltzius after Bartholomäus Spranger). An extremely prolific artist, Bloemaert was also an important teacher who remained open to new ideas. Starting out as a Mannerist, he displayed a Caravaggesque bent with a northern twist by the end of his career. His pupil Honthorst brought the Caravaggesque manner to Utrecht.

Roelant Savery
(Courtrai c. 1576 – Utrecht 1639)

Boar Hunt, 1609
Panel, 24.7 x 35.2 cm – signed and dated – inv. no. 271 – From the Kurfürstliche Galerie (Prince Elector's Gallery)

The climax of the hunt has been reached. Harried by dogs, the mighty boar confronts the hunters, who are on foot. A bearded man is sticking it in the flank with a boar-spear. The wounded animal is trying to escape into the underbrush and the baying dogs are unable to stop him. The second hunter is hidden behind a tree with spear couched and the boar is about to run on to it. The spear staff has fabric or thong twisted round it to afford a secure purchase and the cross-guard prevents the blade from penetrating too deeply into the quarry's flesh so that the hunter will not be left defenceless if he misses his aim. Boar hunting was dangerous. Accuracy of detail and a close-up view focusing on essentials make this picture, for all its small format, a model of its genre. The overall effect is enhanced by subtle handling.

Bartholomäus Spranger
(Antwerp 1546 – Prague 1611)

Angelica and Medoro, c. 1580/85
Canvas, 107.5 x 79.5 cm – inv. no. 10000 – Acquired on the art market in 1935

The motif comes from Ariosto's "Orlando furioso". The lovers are carving their names in the bark of a tree. Spranger painted an entire series of similar love themes for the Emperor Rudolf II. Widespread in engravings, Spranger's style defined Courtly Mannerism.

Hans von Aachen
(Cologne 1552 – Prague 1615)

The Victory of Truth, 1598
Copper, 56 x 47 cm – signed and dated –
inv. no. 1611 – From the Kurfürstliche
Galerie (Prince Elector's Gallery)

Hans Rottenhammer
(Munich 1564 – Augsburg 1625)

Diana and Actaeon, 1602
Copper, 35 x 48 cm – signed and dated –
inv. no. 1588 – From the Kurfürstliche
Galerie (Prince Elector's Gallery)

With the aid of "Justice", the lion, symbol of imperial power, is protecting naked "Truth" against "Deception", which, personified by a bearded man, has already been exposed and brought down. Only when truthfulness reigns, or so the picture tells us, can "Peace", "Prosperity" and "Fertility" thrive in a commonwealth. These qualities are represented by female figures in the middle distance. Political allegories of this type could only flourish under the auspices of a connoisseur and patron of the arts of the stature of the Emperor Rudolf II in Prague. A disarmingly simple line of reasoning is couched in sophisticated visual terms.

Actaeon watched Diana while she was bathing. Discovered, he was turned by the goddess into a stag and punished by being torn by his own hunting dogs. Diana is crouching on the left. One nymph has just caught sight of the transgressor above the grotto while another is trying hastily to cover the goddess' nudity. Although he is as yet unaware of what is happening, antlers are growing out of Actaeon's forehead. Underlying the myth is the ancient idea that mortals who look on deities must die. The theme, here from Ovid's *Metamorphoses*, offered a wealth of possibilities for representing nude figures.

Joseph Heintz the Elder
(Basle 1564 – Prague 1609)

Nymphs and Satyrs, 1599

Copper, oval, 24 x 32 cm – signed and dated – inv. no. 1579 – From the Mannheim Gallery

This is one of the artist's most ingenious pictorial inventions. Creatures associated in myth with the vital powers of nature are depicted amusing themselves. A satyr is blowing pan-pipes and others are listening, drinking, grooming each other and lolling about in pleasant idleness. The story of Pan and Syrinx in Ovid's Metamorphoses may have vaguely inspired the painting. Heintz makes the most of it, creating a charming world of his own. The little copper panel was probably painted for the Emperor Rudolf II. Like Hans von Aachen and Bartholomäus Spranger, Joseph Heintz was active at his court. The oval format, which he knew from Venetian art, corresponds well with the Mannerist ideal of form expressed in the figures and composition.

Adam Elsheimer
(Frankfurt a. Main 1578 – Rome 1610)

The Flight into Egypt, 1609
Copper, 31 x 41 cm – signed and dated – inv. no. 216 – From the Düsseldorf Gallery

A cold night, bathed in bright moonlight, reflected in the still waters of a lake. Against the backdrop of a sombre wood, the Holy Family sets out for Egypt under cover of darkness, fleeing Herod (Mat. 2, 13). Only a small torch lights their path. They are not alone. Standing by off the path with their flocks, shepherds are warming themselves at a fire. This may well be the most hauntingly evocative moonlight night ever painted. Because he prepared his work so carefully and took time with execution, Elsheimer's oeuvre was limited in scope but exerted nonetheless an enormous influence on Baroque painting, including Rubens' work. Elsheimer became friends with him in Rome.

Peter Candid (Pieter de Witte)
(Bruges c. 1548 – Munich 1628)

Duchess Magdalena of Bavaria, c. 1613
Panel, 97.5 x 71.5 cm – inv. no. 2471 – From Scheissheim Castle

The portrait was presumably painted on the occasion of the Duchess' marriage to Duke Wolf-

gang Wilhelm of the Palatinate-Neuburg, which took place on 11 November 1613 in Munich. Magdalena was the youngest daughter of Duke Wilhelm V of Bavaria and a sister of Maximilian, later Prince Elector. The austere magnificence of her attire reveals the influence of Spanish court dress. The sumptuous dress in brilliant red with metallic braid and appliqué decoration, the huge ruff, the heavy tiara, the ornate necklace and big brooch on the red bow all emphasize the sitter's rank. Yet her personality shines through the formal finery. Candid, a pupil of Giorgio Vasari's, came to the Munich court in 1586 after years in the service of the Medici.

Georg Flegel
(Olmütz, Moravia 1566 – Frankfurt 1638)

Grand Banquet Still Life, c. 1630/38
Copper, 78 x 67 cm – signed – inv. no. 1622 – From the Kurfürstliche Gallery (Prince Elector's Gallery)

Flegel made the still life an autonomous genre in Germany. Eating is the principal theme of his extant work: on a table laid for a banquet, in a pantry or, as here, simply on show like a buffet. Flegel's banquets are more than simply a feast for the eyes and the stomach. The unequivocal symbolism underlying these still lifes constitutes a warning against gluttony and vanity. Realism of depiction also discloses a wealth of information on the eating habits, customs and artefacts, in short, the social history of the times.

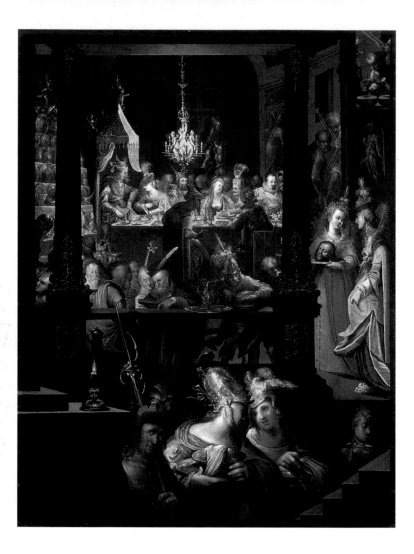

Bartholomäus Strobel the Younger
(Breslau 1591 – Thorn c. 1665 [?])

The Feast of Herod, c. 1625

Canvas, 95 x 73 cm – inv. no. 5120 –
From the Zweibrücken Gallery

Since all his birthday guests raved
about her dancing, Herod told his
step-daughter and niece Salome to
ask for whatever she wished. On
her mother's advice she demanded
the head of John the Baptist, who
was languishing in prison (Mark 6,
21–28).

The artist, who retained a Mannerist style for decades, has created a
painting teeming with details and a
spatial articulation that beggars
description. The play of light is
dazzling and the colours are shrill.
Some of the faces are portraits of
contemporaries.

17th-Century Flemish Painting

Flemish painting forms the core collection of the Alte Pinakothek. The museum is indebted to the 17th and 18th-century Wittelsbachs' passion for collecting and the passage of time, which united the collections amassed by the different branches of the family with works by van Dyck and Jordaens and one of the world's largest Rubens collections. Rubens' illustrious patrons were Duke Wolfgang Wilhelm of the Palatinate-Neuburg and Maximilian I, Prince Elector of Bavaria. Johann Wilhelm of the Palatinate and Max Emanuel, Prince Elector of Bavaria, were among the most committed collectors. The latter acquired the Gisbert van Colen Collection, notable for Rubens' personal portraits. These collections reflect the Counter Reformation, when artists and their patrons renovated churches and furnished them with large altarpieces. Mythology provided material for new galleries and political allegories adorned palaces to enhance the status of monarchy. The Alte Pinakothek also possesses a remarkable collection of Baroque *bozetti*.

Peter Paul Rubens

(Siegen, Westphalia 1577 –
Antwerp 1640)

Rubens and Isabella Brant in a
Honeysuckle Bower, c. 1609

Canvas on panel, 178 x 136.5 cm – inv. no.
334 – From the Düsseldorf Gallery

Immediately after his return from
Italy, Rubens, who was 32, married
18-year-old Isabella Brant. Marking
a new departure in portrait painting, this double portrait was presumably executed not long after the
nuptials. There is no lack of traditional symbolism. Honeysuckle
(woodbine) was a well known symbol of marital fidelity. From ancient
times hands laid one over the other
("dextrarum iunctio") have signified
marriage. Yet all these references
are fully integrated in the realistic
handling and the pose, which captures a moment like a snapshot.
This painting evokes middle-class
contentment, considerable prosperity and conjugal bliss.

Peter Paul Rubens

(Siegen, Westphalia 1577 –
Antwerp 1640)

The Death of Seneca, c. 1612/13

Panel, 185 x 154.7 cm – inv. no. 305 –
From the Düsseldorf Gallery

Accused of treason by his own
pupil, the Emperor Nero, Seneca
was forced to commit suicide. A
physician of his acquaintance
opened his veins and he lay in
warm water to increase the flow of
blood. A scribe is depicted desper-
ately trying to catch the philoso-
pher's last words: "VIR[TUS]" (virtue). The virtue referred to is stoic
compliance with the overall purpose of things, an attitude admira-
bly demonstrated by Seneca in dying. Rubens and his brother Philip
were adherents of Neo-Stoicism.
The painting has something of a
commemorative monument about
it because Rubens used the ancient
statue of an African fisherman,
known in the 17th century as "The
Dying Seneca" as a model. Rubens
also used a portrait bust, the
"pseudo-Seneca", which he owned.

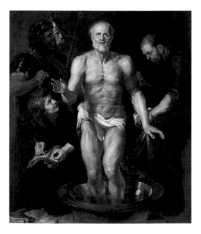

Peter Paul Rubens
(Siegen, Westphalia 1577 –
Antwerp 1640)

Large Last Judgement, 1617
Canvas, 606 x 460 cm – inv. no. 890 –
From the Düsseldorf Gallery

This may be the most overwhelming vision of the end of the world since Michelangelo. Christ appears to judge humanity. Graves have opened and the dead are resurrected to await judgement, separated into the blessed and the damned (Mat. 25, 31-46). Commissioned by Duke Wolfgang Wilhelm of the Palatinate-Neuburg for the high altar of the Jesuit church in Neuburg, it offended contemporary sensibilities. As a result, the monumental work only remained in place for a few decades and even then it was usually draped to hide the nude figures. In 1692 it was moved to the Düsseldorf Gallery.

Peter Paul Rubens
(Siegen, Westphalia 1577 –
Antwerp 1640)

The Battle of the Amazons, c. 1617/18
Panel, 121 x 165 cm – inv. no. 324 –
From the Düsseldorf Gallery

The painting does not represent a
specific battle fought by the Ama-
zons. An ancient race of warrior
women located by Greek mythology in Asia Minor, they were often
involved in conflicts. Here they are
the vanquished, who must flee or
die. Rubens ingeniously exploited
the setting of the scene by dividing
it into two levels. The combatants
swirl about the arched bridge,
which forms the centre-piece of the
action. The view underneath the
bridge lends depth to what is otherwise a relief-like composition.
Rubens' treatment is sketchy yet
fluid handling, ideally suited to
such a turbulent subject. In this
work he was inspired by Leonardo,
Raphael and Titian.

Peter Paul Rubens
(Siegen, Westphalia 1577 –
Antwerp 1640)

Drunken Silenus, c. 1616/17
Panel, 205 x 211 cm – inv. no. 319 –
From the Düsseldorf Gallery

To the strains of the flute and rib-
ald laughter, goat-footed satyrs and
other mythical beings as well as
various animals associated with
Bacchic revels and rustics accompany Dionysus' drunken tutor as
he lurches along trying to keep his

face straight and his heavy legs moving. Rubens may have derived the framing elements of the story from Ovid's Metamorphoses. There Silenus, who has lost his way, is taken by Phrygian peasants to King Midas. Recognizing Silenus at once, the king has a banquet prepared for him. Rubens' representation, however, does not stick to the literary version. Instead, he has drawn on it freely for a symbolic visualisation with a moral: a warning against overindulgence in wine, delivered with a humanist twinkle of the eye. At first conceived with half-length figures, the composition was later enlarged by Rubens himself. The painting hung in Rubens' house in Antwerp.

Peter Paul Rubens and Jan Brueghel

Virgin and Child in a Garland, c. 1616/17

Panel, 185 x 209.8 cm – inv. no. 331 – From the Düsseldorf Gallery

This painting is about the return to devotional images in the Counter-Reformation. A framed "picture in a picture", it recalls a Madonna on a grey house facade garlanded on Church holy days. However the figures are certainly not reproductions from devotional images. Instead, they are depicted in a lively manner, enjoying the decoration. After all, the Virgin is venerated and not the image which refers to her. Rubens left the garland to the skilful brush of his friend "Velvet" Brueghel, the flower specialist. The unusual motif of the Madonna at a cradle occurs in prints before Rubens.

Peter Paul Rubens
(Siegen, Westphalia 1577 –
Antwerp 1640)

**The Rape of the Daughters of
Leucippus, c. 1617/18**
Canvas, 224 x 210.5 cm – inv. no. 321 –
From the Düsseldorf Gallery

Castor and Pollux (Polydeuces), the
sons of Leda and Zeus, abducted
Hilaera and Phoebe, the daughters
of Leucippus, King of Argos, just
before they were to be married.
Lynceus and Idas, the disappointed
grooms, caught the ravishers of
their brides. Idas killed Castor and
Lynceus was accounted for by Polydeuces. Rubens has dealt here with
the first part of the story, which
indeed has voluptuous overtones.
The action is depicted in a courtly
rather than brutal manner. The
ladies are not putting up much
resistance. Abducting young women was sanctioned as a form of
marriage in Laconia and Rubens,

humanist that he was, presumably
knew this. The little amoretti
allude to the sacred precincts of
Aphrodite, where the story was set.
Was the painting commissioned to
celebrate a marriage, perhaps even
double nuptials? Its original purpose is unknown. Rubens brilliant-
ly represents four human figures
and two horses in a composition
which "taxes" the potential of both
picture plane and surface to the full
yet retains a degree of naturalness.
The grouping is a sophisticated choreography. By staggering the planes
in the vertical rather than in the
horizontal and interlocking the figures, the artist has placed them
overwhelmingly close to the picture
plane, thus achieving a breathtaking
monumentality, enhanced by the
low horizon. Parallelism and sym-
metry are deployed to maximum
effect in the arrangement of the
limbs, lending the whole a devastat-
ingly ornamental quality.

Peter Paul Rubens

(Siegen, Westphalia 1577 –
Antwerp 1640)

Lion Hunt, 1621

Canvas, 249 x 377 cm – inv. no. 602 –
Mentioned in 1748 in the Munich Residenz
inventory

Oil sketch for the Lion Hunt, 1621

Panel, 44 x 50 cm – inv. no. 15475 –
Acquired in 1996 with the support of the
Kulturstiftung der Länder (Cultural
Foundation of the Federal States), the
Bayerische Hypotheken- und Wechsel-
bank and the Ernst-von-Siemens-
Kunstfond (Art Endowment Fund)

This dramatic canvas is about life
and death: of both the hunters and
the hunted. Just before the *coup
de grâce* is administered from all
sides, the mighty lion has wrested
a hunter from his mount at the
centre of the painting. The unfor-
tunate man is terrified; another
hunter is already sprawled dead on
the ground. A third is trying vainly
to ward off a second approaching
lion. Rubens was chiefly concerned
with concentrating and distilling
the essence of action. "Grace
and impetuosity" (grâce et
véhémence) are the qualities he
himself mentioned in a letter.
Regarded by Rubens as one of his
best, this painting was commissioned by the English envoy John
Digby as a present for Count
Hamilton.

This sketch represents an early
stage of the overall design, revealing concentration on the dramatic
centre of the pattern. All stages of
execution have been laid down,
from contour drawing to modelling.
A sketch like this gives an exciting
glimpse of the actual process of
creation. On the reverse there is a
design for the Medici Cycle.

Peter Paul Rubens √

(Siegen, Westphalia – 1577 –
Antwerp 1640)

The Fall of the Damned into Hell,
c. 1620

Panel, 288 x 225 cm – inv. no. 320 –
From the Düsseldorf Gallery

The words of the Judge of the
World according to Matthew (25,
41): "Depart from me ye cursed
into everlasting fire, which is prepared for the devil and his angels."
Monstrous figures, lapsed angels
from the dawn of time, attack the
damned even while, caught up in a
powerful vortex, top right, they are
being sucked down into the depths.
Christ, the blessed and the Virgin

and St John as intercessors, who
are otherwise a constituent of Last
Judgements, have been left out, an
iconographic first. It is already too
late for the damned; the Archangel
Michael is executing the sentence
with thunder and lightning. The
dramatic play of shifting light and
colour enhance the horror of the
scene, revealing corpulent bodies in
a blinding flash of brilliance while
others are already being consumed
by the everlasting fire, only to be
extinguished in the depths of the
picture space. The bottom zone,
added later by Rubens, tautens
the composition. A few tortured
faces peer out of the hordes of
condemned as a warning to us.

Peter Paul Rubens

(Siegen, Westphalia 1577 –
Antwerp 1640)

Medici Cycle: The Landing in
Marseille – The Assembly of the
Gods, 1622

Panel, 64 x 50 and 55 x 92 cm – inv. nos.
95 and 103 – From the Kurfürstliche Galerie
(Prince Elector's Gallery)

Between 1621 and 1625 Rubens
completed 24 monumental paintings depicting events from the life
of Maria de' Medici, wife of King
Henry IV of France, who was
assassinated in 1610 (now in the
Louvre). The Alte Pinakothek owns
17 of 25 extant preparatory sketches
in oils. *The Landing in Marseille*
(3 November 1600) depicts the
Queen being welcomed by Francia
(France personified) and Massilia
(Marseille). In *The Assembly of the
Gods* Maria is celebrated as the
peacemaker whose auspicious marriage unites Spain and France.
Apollo and Athena are banishing
Strife and Deception. Rubens has
quoted heavily from ancient litera-
ture here.

As a rule, Rubens made sketches
in oil and submitted them to
patrons who had commissioned
work for approval. The Rubens
workshop executed the paintings
from the sketches and detail studies. Often, and particularly when
several works were commissioned
at once, the preliminary sketches
are all that reveal the master's
own hand.

Peter Paul Rubens

(Siegen, Westphalia 1577 –
Antwerp 1640)

The Woman of the Apocalypse,
1624/25

Canvas, 548 x 365 cm – inv. no. 891 –
Acquired from Freising Cathedral in 1804
during secularization

In the 12th chapter of Revelation,
John describes his vision of "a
woman clothed with the sunne and
the moone was under her feete,
and upon her head a crowne of
twelve starres." She gave birth to a
child menaced by a seven-headed
red dragon. The child was taken up
to God's throne and she fled into
the wilderness. The Archangel
Michael and his hosts appeared
and cast the monster to earth.
The enigmatic motif appears in
numerous variants, some, like
Dürer's, with a winged figure. Its
meanings are also legion: a symbol
of the threatened Church, the
Assumption, the Immaculate Conception. The popularity of the
motif at the time of the Counter-
Reformation needs no explanation.
The painting was commissioned
for the high altar of Freising Cathedral. There is a veduta of the city in
the background.

Peter Paul Rubens
(Siegen, Westphalia 1577 –
Antwerp 1640)

Helene Fourment Dressed as a Bride, c. 1630

Canvas, 163.5 x 136.9 cm – inv. no. 340 –
Acquired by the Prince Elector Max
Emanuel in 1698

Four years after the death of his
first wife (see *The Honeysuckle
Bower*), Rubens married Helene
Fourment, the 16-year-old daughter
of a respected merchant.

Peter Paul Rubens
(Siegen, Westphalia 1577 –
Antwerp 1640)

The Massacre of the Innocents, c. 1636/38

Panel, 199 x 302 cm – inv. no. 572 –
In the Kurfürstliche Galerie (Prince
Elector's Gallery) by 1706

The wholesale slaughter of children in and around Bethlehem
related in Matthew (2, 16–18) is
too terrible for words. It is easier to
describe the composition as a late
Rubens masterpiece. The action
revolves around three main
groups. In each of them ruthless
murder and despair alternate with
brutal killings and furious yet vain
defence. The groups on the left
and right form units. From the
monument to maternal despair
waving a blood-stained cloth at the
centre, one's gaze is directed to the
palace, where Herod is waiting to
hear that his orders have been carried out.

Abraham Janssens
(Antwerp c. 1575 – Antwerp 1632)

The Olympian Gods, c. 1615/20

Canvas, 207 x 240 cm – inv. no. 4884 –
From the Kurfürstliche Galerie (Prince
Elector's Gallery)

The painting can be read like a catalogue of Greek and Roman mythology. Starting from the left: Athena in armour, Hera with a peacock, Zeus with the eagle, Diana with a crescent moon, Apollo with the lyre, Ares in armour (half-concealed), Venus and Cupid (in the foreground) and Hercules with his club. The representation draws on the 10th book of Virgil's *Aeneid*. Venus is standing before the assembled gods to plead for her son, the Trojan Aeneas, on the eve of the Trojan War. Anxious to avoid dissension, Zeus seems to have given up after a short colloquy and will let things take their course. Abraham Janssens is the leading exponent of the "classical" Antwerp School. *The Olympian Gods* reveals Caravaggio's influence in the forceful plasticity achieved by the treatment of light and shade and the crisp contours of the figures. For his motifs Janssen drew on Raphael's Farnesina frescoes. This painting, however, has nothing of Rubens in it although Janssens succumbed to his influence in later years. Meant to be viewed from below, the painting would have originally been hung fairly high on a wall, for example, above a fireplace.

Jacob Jordaens

(Antwerp 1593 – Antwerp 1678)

Allegory of Fecundity, c. 1617

Canvas, 250 x 240 cm – signed – inv. no. 10411 – Acquired on the art market in 1937

Forming a cycle of giving and taking, the figures are crowded up against the picture plane. It is impossible to name individual figures. The figure turned to the left may be Ceres, earth mother and goddess of agriculture. The others, nymphs and satyrs, lend the representation general significance. Nature is bounteous, a theme the artist varied prolifically, approaching it through mythology.

The painting is an early work of Jordaens', executed just two years after he had been accepted as a master in the Antwerp painters' guild. The shrill palette and astonishing glimpses into the depths of the picture space, top left, reveal the twenty-four-year-old artist under the pervasive influence of Mannerism. In his choice of motif, by contrast, he was trendy for his time. After both Rubens and van Dyck were dead, Jordaens still had three productive decades before him.

Jacob Jordaens

(Antwerp 1593 – Antwerp 1678)

**The Satyr and the Peasant,
c. 1620/21**

Canvas on panel, 174 x 206 cm – inv. no.
425 – From the Düsseldorf Gallery

Jordaens executed various versions
of the Aesop fable. A satyr visits a
peasant and is so annoyed to find
the latter first blowing on his
hands to warm them and then on
his soup to cool it that he flees the
house.

Since the story is supposed to
convey a moral message, a warning against the duplicity of people
who sound friendly and mean un-
kindness, the satyr looks more
like a staid pedagogue than a skit-
tish mythical being.

Sir Antony van Dyck

(Antwerp 1599 – London 1641)

Self-portrait, c. 1621/22

Canvas, 82.5 x 70.2 cm – inv. no. 405 –
From the Düsseldorf Gallery

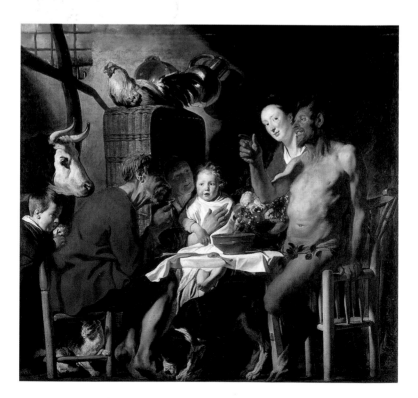

The painter had just turned twenty when he painted this early self-portrait. Gazing out of the picture, he is also directing a searching look at himself. As young as he seems, the painter was already very aware of the importance of formal appearance. Contemporaneous descriptions of him paint a picture of a young man who went about looking more like a noble than a bourgeois and was always elegantly dressed. The gold chain, probably a present from Duke Fernando Gonzaga, was added later when the artist worked over the painting and enlarged it.

Sir Antony van Dyck
(Antwerp 1599 – London 1641)

Portrait of Filips de Godines, 1627/32

Canvas, 211.5 x 137.6 cm – inv. no. 995 – From the Kurfürstliche Galerie (Prince Elector's Gallery)

The sitter (1603–1633), son of a Portuguese merchant, was a tax gatherer for the Spanish king. He is portrayed with one foot on a step, which makes his massive figure surprisingly lively and forceful. There is a companion piece, a portrait of his wife, Sebilla van den Berghe (not reproduced here).

Sir Antony van Dyck

(Antwerp 1599 – London 1641)

Susanna and the Elders, c. 1622/23

Canvas, 194 x 144 cm – inv. no. 595 –
From the Düsseldorf Gallery

What the Bible (Daniel 13) dwells on at length has here been condensed to evocative gestures and glances: Susanna's fright, the lust of the old men forced on her, the spider-like hand pawing at her shoulder which gives her the creeps, the nastily avuncular approach and the pretended severity of the younger man, brashly grabbing her towel. A clear case of sexual harassment, which, due to the young woman's steadfastness of character and the intervention of young, quick-witted Daniel, will end happily, with the Elders found guilty and punished. Here van Dyck reveals his brilliance as a storyteller with a psychological bent. He is able to empathize with the situation from both the masculine and the feminine viewpoint. The story of Susanna surprised in her bath was often represented as an example of virtue triumphant.

Sir Antony van Dyck

(Antwerp 1599 – London 1641)

The Lamentation, 1634

Panel, 108.7 x 149.3 cm – monogrammed
and dated – inv. no. 606 – From the
Düsseldorf Gallery

Seated on the ground, the Virgin is holding up by the torso and legs the body of her son, which has been taken down from the cross. In a voiceless lament and with no tears left to shed, she lifts up her face to reveal swollen, reddened eyes. Her gesture is demonstratively sacrificial. Angels and cherubim mourn with her. The cross, the crown of thorns and the gory nails in the foreground invite the viewer to meditate on the Passion. The artist has "summed up mariology" here, with the emphasis on the Virgin's intercessory function. The striking pose taken by the figure of Christ at his mother's breast pre-sumably made van Dyck's contemporaries think of the "bundle of myrrhe" of the Song of Solomon, "who shall lie betweene my breasts" (SS 1, 12), a widely popular motif which had been linked with the sufferings of the Virgin for centuries. In placing the cross obliquely, the artist extends this thought, using it as a sophisticated device for evoking the impression that the cross and its burden are resting on the Virgin's shoulders. This is an expression of the idea, familiar to the Baroque period, that the mother's compassionate sufferings gave her a share in the Redemption of humanity (co-redemptio). Formally this unusual composition derives from Michelangelo engravings although the handling and palette recall Titian. Sketchy brushwork in some parts contrasts with the modulated plasticity of Christ's body on the white cloth.

Frans II Francken
(Antwerp 1581 – Antwerp 1642)

Banquet in the House of Burgomaster Rockox, c. 1630/35

Panel, 62.3 x 96.5 cm – signed – inv. no. 858 – From the Düsseldorf Gallery

During the 17th century Flemish painters specialized in representations for private galleries. Francken, a leading exponent of the genre, presents the reception room in Nicolas Rockox's house. He was burgomaster of Antwerp nine times. His walls are adorned with art, some of it, such as the ancient portrait busts and the following paintings, identifiable and even recorded in the inventory of the patrician's estate: Rubens' *Samson and Delilah*, Jan Sanders van Hemessen's *St Jerome*, Marinus van Reymerswaele's *Money-Changers* and Quenten Massys' *Saviour*. Whereas the furnishings, appointments and decoration of the interior are probably true to life, the staffage figures are possibly fig-ments of the painter's imagination, representing the five senses. The door into the next room is open to reveal the *Doubting Thomas* Rubens painted for the Rockox mortuary chapel in 1613/15. In view of the riches displayed in the foreground, might this be a subtle reminder of the transience of earthly things?

Adriaen Brouwer
(Oudenaarde 1605/06 – Antwerp 1638)

The Sense of Taste, c. 1635

Panel, 23.7 x 20.5 cm – monogrammed – inv. no. 626 – In 1748 in the "Flamändisches Cabinet" in Schleissheim

Adriaen Brouwer specialized in genre paintings of peasants in small formats. His handling was sophisticated and his work lively. Here he has reverted in a tavern scene to the time-honoured tradition of five-senses pictures. Even in those days people knew that smoking was bad for your health. "The intoxication of tobacco" was condemned then as it is today. To see how good it can taste, though, just take a look at the rapt expression on the face of the man at the table, who is savouring the smoke curling up from his mouth.

Adriaen Brouwer
(Oudenaarde 1605/06 – Antwerp 1638)

Village Barber-Shop, c. 1631

Panel, 31.4 x 39.6 cm – monogrammed – inv. no. 561 – From the Düsseldorf Gallery

In 1631 Brouwer moved from Haarlem or Amsterdam to Antwerp. This painting dates from just after the move. The village barber was all things to all men – barber, quack and surgeon. Here he is operating on a foot. His assistant is sterilizing the knife for the next patient on a little stove. The individual motifs so reminiscent of still lifes, the precise rendering of fabric textures and the portrayal of emotions are particularly striking in surroundings that are depicted in a subdued palette.

David Teniers the Younger

(Brussels 1610 – Brussels 1690)

Tavern Scene, c. 1639/40

Panel, 37.3 x 52.8 cm – inv. no. 818 – From
the Kurfürstliche Galerie (Prince Elector's
Gallery)

Teniers was one of Adriaen
Brouwer's most successful followers. However, unlike Brouwer, who
died young, Teniers had a long
active working life spanning nearly
a century. The *Tavern Scene* is a
mature work. By the time Brouwer
died, Teniers had lightened his palette and his treatment of light had
become more uniform. This work,
too, is modelled on Brouwer, as
numerous quotes from him
show.

Teniers painted landscapes, har-
vest scenes and fairs as well as
genre scenes set in taverns. In
1651 he became Court Painter to
the Spanish stadholder, Grand
Duke Leopold Wilhelm. Teniers
was the most successful genre
painter in the southern Netherlands and his work was in demand
throughout Europe.

17th-Century Dutch Painting

Holland was originally merely one of seven northern provinces of the Netherlands which had liberated themselves from the Spanish-dominated south in 1568. Calvinism, which eschewed visual imagery, gave the art of Holland a distinctive character, notably different from that of the Catholic region. The Church was not a patron of the arts in the north. Nevertheless, the growing prosperity of the mercantile class in the "Golden Age" gave rise to a love of art for its own sake. Connoisseurs promoted painters who worked to exacting standards of quality many artists specialized in particular genres. The subjects painted drew on empirical knowledge of reality often with underlying, moralizing themes. Formats were small, suitable for hanging in private homes. Rembrandt is magnificently represented in the Alte Pinakothek with extraordinary paintings, among them a youthful self-portrait, *The Raising of the Cross* and *The Deposition*. These paintings came from the Düsseldorf, Mannheim and Zweibrücken Galleries.

Esaias van de Velde

(Amsterdam c. 1591 –
The Hague 1630)

Ice-Skating on the Town Moat, 1618

Panel, 29.8 x 50.4 cm – signed and dated –
inv. no. 2884 – From the Zweibrücken
Gallery

Esaias van de Velde's work marks a
leap forward in Dutch landscape
painting. A comparison with Jan
Brueghel's *Large Fishmarket*,
painted just fifteen years before,
shows that idealized landscape
composition has yielded to reality
as actually seen. The separation of
the picture ground into zones
marked by differing tonality has
been replaced by a unified picture
space flooded with light which the
viewer's eye is free to trace to the
horizon. The palette has been
reduced to create atmospheric
effects. In its subtle tonality, it
anticipates the distinctive monochrome landscapes of van de
Velde's pupil, Jan van Goyen.

Paulus Moreelse

(Utrecht 1571 – Utrecht 1638)

Blonde Shepherdess, 1624

Canvas, 76.1 x 63.2 cm – monogrammed
and dated – inv. no. 13183 – From the
Düsseldorf Gallery

Baroque pastoral scenes are peopled with idealized figures of shepherds and shepherdesses drawn
from real life. The presumed (erotic) licence associated with rustic
life fascinated the urban middle
classes.

Pieter Lastman
(Amsterdam 1583 – Amsterdam 1633)

Odysseus and Nausicaa, 1619

Panel, 91.5 x 117.2 cm – monogrammed and dated – inv. no. 4947 – Acquired by the Prince Elector Karl Theodor in 1792

The scene represented is based on the Odyssey (6th book). Off Scyrus, the island of the Phaeacians, Poseidon has smashed the raft made by Odysseus to sail home on after his adventure with Calypso. The Greek hero swims to shore, where he meets Nausicaa, daughter of King Alcinous, who is doing the washing on the beach with her companions. Given a warm welcome at court, Odysseus is eventually equipped with a new boat so that he can continue his voyage home.

Lastman shows Nausicaa surprised yet calmly greeting the supplicant on the beach while her companions scatter into flight at the sight of a naked man. Depicting a scene and its protagonists clearly and unequivocally is what Lastman's pictorial idiom is all about. Expressive gestures convey characterisation and narrate action. A bright palette and a dramatically ordered composition enhance the two protagonists' stature. The viewer observes the scene at Odysseus' eye-level. Despite the panic around her, Nausicaa is calmly authoritative. Her eyes seek contact with Odysseus' to form a diagonal emerging from the depths of the picture space and crossing the stagy staggering of planes on which the fleeing companions are represented, thus locking the composition into a taut mirror inversion that fully exploits the picture space. In abandoning the Mannerist principles which dominated history painting, Lastman laid the foundations on which his pupil Rembrandt built.

Gerrit van Honthorst
(Utrecht 1590 – Utrecht 1656)

Conviviality, 1622

Canvas, 130 x 195.6 cm – signed and dated
– inv. no. 1312 – From the Düsseldorf
Gallery

"Gherardo della Notte" ("Gerard
of the Night Scenes") made his
name with night pieces. In 1620
he introduced Caravaggesque *chiaroscuro* to northern painting,
exerting a decisive influence on
the Utrecht School. In *Conviviali-
ty* and in numerous other works,
the light-and-shade effects are
achieved by natural means. Can-
dlelight enabled light values to be
subtly varied on the grey scale
from blinding lightness to deep
black. The subject of the painting,
which has admonitory moral
overtones (the inevitable personal
and social consequences of
drunkenness), developed out
of the parable of the Prodigal
Son.

Frans Hals
(Antwerp 1582/83 – Haarlem 1666)

Portrait of Willem van Heythuysen,
c. 1625

Canvas, 204.5 x 134.5 cm – inv. no. 14101
– Acquired in 1969 from the Liechten-
stein Collection, Vaduz

Willem van Heythusen had
attained considerable affluence
in the yarn trade in Haarlem.
Posed in an opulently over-dram-
atized Baroque setting, he is
dressed in his best and appears
arrogantly self-confident. For all
his grandeur, however, wilting
roses on the floor symbolize the
limits of earthly riches. A pious
Calvinist, van Heythuysen put his
fortune to good use by endowing
two almshouses with his estate.
One of them is still operating in
Haarlem.

Frans Hals

*(Antwerp 1582/83 –
Haarlem 1666)*

**Portrait of Willem Croes,
c. 1662/66**

Panel, 47.1 x 34.4 cm – inv. no. 8402 –
monogrammed –
Acquired in 1906

Sketchy handling makes this late masterpiece of the painter's distinctive. The brushwork is additive; the articulation of surfaces is merely suggested and some parts even appear to have remained unfinished. Yet, viewed from a distance, the authoritative figure of this assertive bourgeois develops an astonishing degree of plasticity. Willem Croes, a

brewer in Haarlem, died in 1666, just three weeks before the artist.

Rembrandt Harmensz. van Rijn
(Leiden 1606 – Amsterdam 1669)

Self-portrait, 1629

Panel, 15.5 x 12.7 cm – monogrammed and dated – inv. no. 11427 – Acquired in 1953 from the Herzoglich Sachsen-Coburg Gotha'sche Familienstiftung (Ducal Saxon-Coburg Gotha Endowment)

No bigger than a man's hand, this is a self-portrait of the artist at the age of twenty-three. In half-profile, it seems spontaneous, captured, as it were, in passing. The rather shy look in the subject's dark eyes seems questioning. His mouth is open as if he is about to speak. Light falls steeply from above left, touching his cheek and bulbous nose and making his white collar glow. The collar itself is a tour de force of fluid yet impasted brushwork. Rembrandt saved himself the trouble of delineating his tousled locks. He simply scratched with the butt end of his brush through the paint while it was still wet right down to the panel support. No other painter before or since has painted so many self-portraits as Rembrandt. Looking out of one's self-portrait means literally and figuratively looking at oneself reflected in a mirror.

Rembrandt Harmensz. van Rijn
(Leiden 1606 – Amsterdam 1669)

The Deposition, 1633

Panel, 89.4 x 65.2 cm – signature spurious – inv. no. 395 – From the Düsseldorf Gallery

A harsh cone of light hits the five men who are straining to take down the body of Christ from the cross. There is nothing left of beauty in the corpse (Isaiah 53, 2: "neither forme nor beautie"). The skin is pale and flabby and the limbs hang down heavily and limply, causing the labourers a great deal of trouble. Compare Rubens' idealized figures of Christ with this one! The figure dressed in bright blue, who also appears in the companion piece, *The Raising of the Cross*, is a self-portrait of the artist. The rest of the scene is extinguished in darkness. On the left the swooning Virgin is being cared for by the women with her. The painting is part of a series of five commissioned by the Stadholder, Frederick Henry of Orange.

Rembrandt Harmensz. van Rijn
(Leiden 1606 – Amsterdam 1669)

The Holy Family, c. 1633/34

Canvas, 183.5 x 123 cm – signed and (partly illegibly) dated – inv. no. 1318 – From the Mannheim Gallery

The Holy Family had never before been represented in such a down-to-earth, humane manner. The Christ Child has fallen contentedly asleep at his mother's breast. Full of fatherly pride and joy, Joseph stoops gently over the child. Mary, still rocking him, is leaning towards Joseph without looking at him. She is cradling the child's feet in loving hands to warm them. The sophisticated treatment of light and differentiated handling emphasize what is important. In containing the group within the contour of a tilted oval, Rembrandt found the ideal form for the scene.

Rembrandt Harmensz. van Rijn (Workshop of)

The Sacrifice of Isaac, 1636

Canvas, 195 x 132.3 cm – signed – inv. no. 438 – From the Mannheim Gallery

A cruel test of his faith awaits Abraham, the Hebrew patriarch. He is to sacrifice his only son. However, an angel intervenes at the last minute to prevent the deed (Gen. 22, 1-13). The painting is presumably the work of a pupil with corrections by Rembrandt himself because the inscription "Rembrandt verandert. En over geschildert" is on the lower edge. In the first version in St Petersburg (1635), the angel emerges from the left. Here he is depicted as dramatically thrusting forward from out of the picture space in a manner requiring far more sophisticated handling of perspective.

Rembrandt Harmensz. van Rijn
(Leiden 1606 – Amsterdam 1669)

Christ Risen, 1661

Canvas, 78.5 x 63 cm – signed and dated (spurious?) – inv. no. 64/1 – From the collection of the Provost of Mainz Cathedral, Hugo Franz, Count Eltz

At some time the canvas was considerably cut down. Christ probably grasped the staff of the cross or a banner in his left hand.

Jan van Goyen
(Leiden 1596 – The Hague 1656)

Farmsteads on a River, 1636

Panel, 39.5 x 60 cm – signed and dated – inv. no. 4893 – From the Fürstbischöfliche Galerie (Prince-Bishop's Gallery), Würzburg

Wind-battered farmhouses and a dove-cote perched on high piles are clustered on a river bank amidst knotty trees. The men who live here are fishing. The mood is one of peaceful plenty. On the untroubled surface of the water, the mirror-image unobtrusively reflects the harmony of man and nature. In his landscapes van Goyen was not concerned with the faithful rendering of topographical detail. Travelling through the countryside, he made a lot of drawings which he used as studies for paintings. The monochrome palette prevailing throughout was deliberately achieved under studio conditions.

Pieter Jansz. Saenredam
(Assendelft 1597 – Haarlem 1665)

**Interior of St James's Church,
Utrecht, 1642**

Panel, 55.2 x 43.4 cm – signed and dated –
inv. no. 6622 – From the Fürstbischöfliche
Galerie (Prince-Bishop's Gallery),
Würzburg

Church interiors are a specialized
genre in Dutch painting. They are
often depicted as empty (Calvinist
churches are without devotional
images). There may be a pulpit,
an organ and even a few figures
or, as here, the funerary plaques
of Utrecht families. Paintings of
this kind are documentary "portraits of architecture". Saenredam
always made meticulous preliminary sketches, which were precisely dated. His drawing of St
James's were made six years (12
August 1636) before the painting.
During his stay in Utrecht, a
Plague epidemic took a toll of
thousands. Is this why the artist
chose to put his signature com-
memoratively on one of the
funerary plaques?

Carel Fabritius
(Midden-Beemster 1622 – Delft 1654)

Self-portrait, c. 1650

Canvas, 62.5 x 51 cm – monogrammed – inv. no. 2080 – From the Fürstbischöfliche Galerie (Prince Bishop's Gallery), Würzburg

Emulating his teacher, Rembrandt, the painter has portrayed himself in exotic costume. The most talented of the master's many pupils, Fabritius did not live long enough to leave more than a small oeuvre. Nevertheless, it exerted a strong influence on the Delft painters Jan Vermeer and Pieter de Hooch. At thirty-two Fabritius was killed when the Delft municipal powder magazine blew up. He chose his surname to show he had trained as a carpenter (Lat. faber, meaning "maker"). Quite a few critics have attributed this portrait to Barent Fabritius, Carel's brother, who was also a pupil of Rembrandt's.

Willem Kalf
(Rotterdam 1619 – Amsterdam 1693)

Still Life with a Porcelain Jug, 1653

Panel, 44.9 x 35.7 cm – signed and dated – inv. no. 10763 – Acquired in 1940 on the Berlin art market

After an interlude in Paris, Willem Kalf moved from Rotterdam to Amsterdam in 1650, where he stayed for the rest of his life. There he gradually perfected the grand Baroque still life although, while in Paris, he had also executed genre scenes of rustic life. This still life with a porcelain jug is the artist's earliest dated work after his move to Amsterdam. Typical of Kalf's mature work is the way sophisticated arrangements of precious objects and fruit glow in subtle colour out of darkness. The play of light configures surface textures – porcelain, glass, fruits and metal – with exquisite economy.

Philips Koninck
(Amsterdam 1619 – Amsterdam 1688)

Flats Landscape, c. 1653/55

Canvas, 133.3 x 165.7 cm – inv. no. 9407 –
Acquired in 1927 from an art dealer

The sky takes up two thirds of the picture. Clouds are the subject here, driven by winds, probably after a heavy rainfall, black and heavy, tattered yet still towering banks of cumulus. Patches of blue shine through; the weather will clear ("enough blue to make a Dutchman a pair of breeches"). Viewed from high up, the landscape is built on the shifting light, shade and half-shade of swiftly moving clouds. Strips of trees and bushes, whose roots secure the flats against the incursions of the sea, articulate the picture plane. A meandering ditch creates a diagonal in contrasting ochrous reflection, counterbalanced by the dull glint of grey water in the middle distance. Not much is happening. In the foreground a fisherman is casting and in the middle distance a shepherd is driving his flock. You hardly notice the village with its high church spire. This is not a colourful landscape. The vegetation is silvery grey, the ground ochre and the clouds and water are in subtle tones of grey and white. In the foreground, the subdued watery palette condenses to the clayey ochre of the bank, laid on with a loaded brush. One of the greatest masters of the genre, Koninck drew on empirical observation to create the ideal type of Dutch landscape.

Abraham van Beyeren

(The Hague 1620/21 – Overschie 1690)

Large Still Life with Lobster, 1653

Canvas, 125.5 x 105 cm – monogrammed and dated – inv. no. 1620 – From the Mannheim Gallery

This grand Baroque still life is a sumptuous display of luxury goods, both edible and collectable. Stagily arranged on a dark green velvet cloth in front of a silk curtain caught up on a thin rod, conspicuous consumption is given its due. The column and landscape vista are pathos conventions underscoring the artificiality of the whole. Seeming disarray is a stylistic device fundamental to the genre. The knocked-over goblet, the heavy white napkin slipping off the table and the silver salver perched precariously on the edge are supposed to lend an air of spontaneity. The pocket watch placed at the edge of the table on the right suggests that time flies and that all earthly goods are perishable. With his theatrical stage setting van Beyeren is quoting Flemish models.

Gerard ter Borch (Terborch)
(Zwolle 1617 – Deventer 1681)

A Letter Spurned, c. 1655/58

Panel, 55.9 x 46.5 cm – signed – inv. no. 206 – From the Kurfürstliche Galerie (Prince Elector's Gallery)

A courier approaches submissively, holding out a letter yet the lady gives him short shrift, pretending that this is just an unwelcome intrusion on her morning toilette. You know she's about to take the letter and devour its contents. Of course it's a love letter. The pained and questioning expression on the maid's face reveals that she knows how long her mistress has been awaiting this missive. Gerard ter Borch painted both portraits and genre scenes in domestic settings. The latter are restrained works which narrate entire stories through evocative gestures, expressive glances or the mere intimation of action. As this painting shows, ter Borch's powers of observation of human frailties are matched by masterly execution. Genre scenes of this type build on the rendering of textures, particularly silk, whose surface breaks up the light into a myriad of reflections. In this painting, however, the courier's soft, woolly clothing is what catches the eye. The handling here centres on action and indeed the centre of the scene is more precisely rendered than what is peripheral to it.

Gerard ter Borch (Terborch)
(Zwolle 1617 – Deventer 1681)

Boy Fleaing His Dog, c. 1655
Canvas, 34.4 x 27.1 cm – monogrammed –
inv. no. 589 – From the Düsseldorf Gallery

The long-suffering dog is looking soulfully and rather coyly at us while the boy concentrates on purposefully combing through its coat with his fingers for fleas. If he catches one, he'll squeeze it with great gusto.

The room is sparingly furnished. A dog-eared schoolboy's copybook, closed and out of the way, is lying on a three-legged desk hewn from a log. A pen sticks out of an inkwell with its case neatly arranged next to it. The foreground is furnished with a low stool. The felt hat on it is at once a repoussoir, creating depth, and a painterly tour de force.

The message of the painting is ambivalent. Does it symbolize domestic order, which also extends to caring for pets, or is it a warning against wasting time on distracting pursuits (when one should be doing homework, for instance)? The appealing motif has been copied over and over again. As early as 1510 Lucas van Leyden did a copperplate engraving of a dog-fleaing scene but ter Borch's rendering does not seem to refer to it.

Philips Wouwerman (Wouwermans)
(Haarlem 1619 – Haarlem 1668)

Winter Landscape with Skaters,
c. 1655

Panel, 47.6 x 63.7 cm – signed – inv. no.
152 – From the Zweibrücken Gallery

Hunting scenes, battle scenes, the arrival and departure of travellers – horses are always there in Wouwerman's landscapes. A grey is the hallmark of this particular painter, encountered in much of his work. This winter landscape is no exception. The grey's shiny, blueish harness looks stylish with the elegant dragon sledge. Like the black horse galloping beside him, he seems to be pulling people from the upper ranks of society for the oncoming couple is greeting them respectfully. On the left the lower orders are enjoying themselves. A man has opened up a tavern in a tent. Grown-ups are drinking while children are playing "kolf" and skating. The painter presumably spent most of his life in Haarlem. He trained under his father, whose work is unknown. Later he worked for a while in Frans Hals's Haarlem workshop. Although landscape is emphasized in the work done by Wouwerman in the 1640s, peopled by staffage figures, with maturity he grew to attach more importance to figures, placing them in the foreground of his paintings. Wouwerman was extremely prolific. About 800 paintings executed over a period of 30 years are attributed to him. He was particularly appreciated in the 18th century.

Willem van de Velde the Younger
(Leiden 1633 – Westminster 1707)

Calm Sea, c. 1655
Canvas, 51.6 x 56.5 cm – inv. no. 1032 –
From the collection of King Max I

There is an unreal quality about this painting. Two fishing smacks are at anchor in the foreground. They are reflected on the surface of the utterly still water. There is no wind at all. Heavy clouds seem to weight down the sky in the middle distance but haze unites it with the sea at the horizon. Calm and balanced, the composition is masterly and the palette reticent yet subtle. The symbolic content of this masterpiece is fairly obvious. The allegory of "waiting for the right moment" can be taken as a guideline for living.

Marine painting was a specialist genre in 17th-century Holland and Willem van de Velde one of its greatest masters. He trained first under his father, Willem van de Velde the Elder, and later under Simon de Vlieger. From 1672/73 both he and his father were in the service of Charles II of England. Not all van de Velde paintings are as peaceful as *Calm Sea. Ships in a Storm* was also in demand as a motif on both sides of the Channel. Drawing on his expert knowledge of ships and rigging, he painted almost documentary pieces of sea-battles between England and Holland, selling his work on both markets.

Adriaen van Ostade
(Haarlem 1610 – Haarlem 1685)

Rustics Brawling, 1656

Panel, 44.8 x 37.4 cm – signed and dated – inv. no. 566 – From the Düsseldorf Gallery

The brawl is in full swing and no one knows what started it in the first place. Peasants are going at each other with clubs, stools and fists. A combatant on the right has drawn his knife and his wife and child are hard put to constrain him.

Ostade is a leading exponent of rustic Dutch genre painting. Adriaen Brouwer, with whom he worked in Frans Hals's studio, exerted a formative influence on him. Urban bourgeois collectors and even foreign nobles were among his clientele. Much of his work is close to caricature but it always contains a genially counterbalancing element. The Alte Pinakothek owns another Ostade from the same period as well as a pair of paintings in the cool, light palette and precision of detail characteristic of his early work.

Jacob van Ruisdael
(Haarlem 1628/29 – Amsterdam 1682)

View of Ootmarsum, 1660/70

Canvas, 59.1 x 73.2 cm – spurious
signature – inv. no. 10818 – Acquired in
1942 from the collection of Prince Ernst
of Saxony-Meiningen

Nicolaes Berchem
(Haarlem 1620 – Amsterdam 1683)

Italian Landscape in Evening Light, c. 1670

Panel, 41.2 x 54.5 cm – signed – inv. no.
266 – From the Kurfürstliche Galerie
(Prince Elector's Gallery)

The view is from Kuiperberg hill with the medieval church dominating the centre. Houses with brilliant red tile roofs are clustered about it. The windmill is the only element other than the church to break the horizon. The outlines of Bentheim Castle are vaguely discernible in the distance. Two thirds of the picture plane are taken up by the sky. Three large masses of cloud sweep up from the horizon to distribute sunlight across the landscape. The work was painted in the artist's studio from drawings he made in the 1650s.

The reddish light of the setting sun suffuses a river valley and mountains, which are sinking into the haze of evening and darkness. The treatment of light is only one attractive feature of this painting. Another is the contrast between the landscape and the clearly delineated, three-dimensional figures of the shepherds. Berchem, the son of the still-life painter Pieter Claesz, probably spent time between 1651 and 1653 in Italy. Highly prolific, he is the leading exponent of the Dutch Italianate landscape, with 850 paintings extant.

Jan Steen
(Leiden 1625/26 – Leiden 1679)

Love-Lorn, c. 1660

Canvas, 61 x 52.1 cm – signed – inv. no. 158 – From the Düsseldorf Gallery

Showing a great deal of sympathy with her plight, the physician is taking the lady's pulse. She looks up at him pale and forlorn. The older woman looks unsympathetic and knowing. A scrap of paper in the love-sick lady's hand bears the diagnosis: "Daar baat geen / mede-syn / want het is / minepyn" ("There is no remedy for the pangs of love"). The Cupid atop the wind-breaker has hit the mark. A popular motif in genre painting, the doctor's visit has been presented ironically by Steen. At least 20 versions of the subject are known from his hand. His rendering of details and particularly fabric textures, is masterly.

Frans van Mieris
(Leiden 1635 – Leiden 1681)

Lady before a Looking-Glass, c. 1670

Panel, 43 x 31.5 cm, round top converted into a rectangle – inv. no. 219 – From the Kurfürstliche Galerie (Prince Elector's Gallery)

Mieris and his teacher, Gerard Dou, made Leiden famous for highly polished genre painting of domestic scenes. With the precision of a miniaturist, this skilled colourist was in control of every square inch of his little paintings. Here the subject is not so fine. The lady is so overdressed that she may be a harlot; her searching glance at her reflection may anticipate sinful behaviour. The moral message is ambivalent. The mirror is the tool of vanity but it is also a means to self-knowledge leading to betterment.

Jacob van Ruisdael
(Haarlem 1628 – Amsterdam 1682)

Oaks along a Torrent, 1670s
Canvas on panel, 71.7 x 90.1 cm – signature probably spurious – inv. no. 1038 – From the estate of King Max I

A rickety plank bridge crosses the raging torrent from the foreground to a grove of oaks in the middle distance. A peasant family is resting under them. In the background, right, there is a village. Only the church spire and the mill on the outskirts rise above the houses. Clouds swollen with rain suggest that the weather may change any minute. Ruisdael's figures are always small and insignificant, subordinated to the natural setting. The painting is an allegory of life. The birch in the foreground, which may have been hit by lightning, the dead branches on the otherwise sturdy oaks and the hollow trunk in front of them are reminders that death is part of life. The stream and the weather show that the elements are unpredictable. Finally, the rickety footbridge symbolizes man's hazardous way through life.

Ruisdael is the most important landscape painter of the latter half of the century. His influence on 19th-century painting was considerable. Moreover, Ruisdael was not just a painter. He studied medicine and worked for a time as a surgeon in Amsterdam. In 1676 he is said to have taken a medical degree at Caen. Art as a second profession is no rarity in Dutch painting.

Adriaen van der Werff

(Kralingen 1659 – Rotterdam 1722)

Children Playing before a Hercules Group, 1687

Panel, 46.8 x 35 cm – signed and dated –
inv. no. 250 – From the Düsseldorf Gallery

Porcelain gloss and a cool, enamel-like finish made Adriaen van der Werff's meticulously executed paintings hot collector's items in their day at European courts. In 1697 Johann Wilhelm, the Wittelsbach Elector Palatine, succeeded in inducing the artist to become his Court Painter.

This little painting conveys its message gracefully. Antithetical groups in the foreground and middle distance illustrate a warning to young people not to waste their precious time on useless pursuits. Hercules' battle against vice is the motto of the piece.

17th and 18th-Century Italian Painting

The selection of Italian Baroque painting in the Alte Pinakothek is relatively small, reflecting the Neo-Classical preferences of King Ludwig I, who founded the Alte Pinakothek. To counterbalance what may seem a deficiency, the Staatsgalerien in Schleissheim and Würzburg have given more space to Italian Baroque painting, which represents a current running counter to Late Mannerism, a period style scarcely present at all in the Alte Pinakothek. The driving force behind Italian Baroque was retrograde, a not uncommon phenomenon in art. In this case, it entailed a return to the Italian High Renaissance. The Carraccis of Bologna mark the beginning of this revival. Caravaggio's innovative genius is only indirectly at work in the Alte Pinakothek (represented by followers, the Caravaggisti). Moreover, for a long time there was a dearth of 18th-century painting in the Alte Pinakothek. The Bayerische Hypotheken- und Wechsel-bank has taken the lead since the 1960s in adding substantially to the collection.

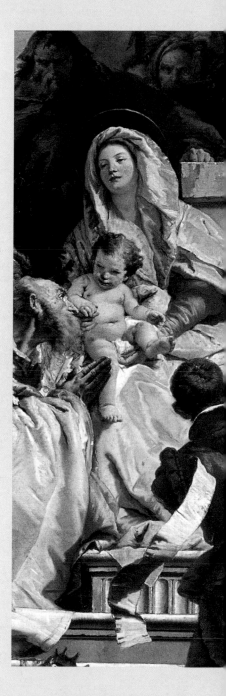

Federigo Barocci
(Urbino 1535 – Urbino 1612)

Christ and St Mary Magdalene
(Noli me tangere), 1590

Canvas, 259 x 185 cm – signed and dated –
inv. no. 494 – From the Düsseldorf Gallery

In the light of dawn, Christ
speaks to the mourner at the
empty tomb after the Resurrection. At first she thinks he is a
gardener. Not until he addresses
her by name does she recognize
him. Mary Magdalene gazes at
him fondly, caught in an almost
girlish gesture of embarrassment
as she has turned towards him.
Christ's words "Noli me tangere"
("Touch me not") to her indicate
his transfigured state. He charges
her with telling the disciples of
their encounter (John 20, 11-17).
This work is distinctive as a telling representation of a psycho-
logically complex situation.
Barocci developed his style,
marking a transition from Mannerism to Baroque, by studying
the work of Raphael, Titian and
Correggio.

Carlo Saraceni

(Venice c. 1580/85 – Venice 1620)

The Vision of St Francis, c. 1620

Canvas, 242 x 165 cm – signed – inv. no.
113 – Recorded in Schleissheim from 1748

The scene represented is St Francis
being comforted by a music-making angel. The saint was blind in
the closing years of his life. The
event took place in 1225 in Rieti at
the house of a man with the same
surname as the artist, the Canon

Tebaldo Sarraceni. The angel's colourful robe contrasts sharply and
auspiciously with the sickroom,
which has been rendered in a sombre yet saturated palette. Colour
conveys the experience of music.
The treatment of light and the naturalistic representation of objects
reveal the influence of the Roman
Caravaggisti. The painting was
probably purchased in 1620 for the
Bavarian Duke and later Prince
Elector, Maximilian I.

Johann Liss
(Oldenburger Land c. 1597 –
Venice 1629/30)

The Death of Cleopatra, c. 1622/24

Canvas, 97.5 x 85.5 cm – inv. no. 13434 –
Acquired in 1964

Cleopatra, Queen of Egypt and
mistress of Mark Antony, the
Roman statesman and general,
committed suicide by allowing an
asp to bite her to avoid being tak-
en prisoner by Octavian (later the
Emperor Augustus). Liss developed a style inspired by Flemish,
Roman and Venetian painting yet
nonetheless distinctively his own.
With the fluidly broad brushwork
evident in his rendering of fabrics
and the supple configurations of
surface composition, the painter
was far ahead of his time. These
stylistic features are not encountered again until Rococo.

Orazio Gentileschi
(Pisa 1563 – London 1639)

Martha Reproving Mary, c. 1620

Canvas, 133 x 155 cm – inv. no. 12726 –
Given to the museum in 1957

The title given traditionally to the
painting after Luke 10, 38–42
may be spurious. This is probably
a representation with a moral
message contrasting vanity and
modesty. Pointing out her failings
to the girl whose attributes are
loose blonde hair and a mirror, the
virtuous girl wearing a headscarf
gestures urgently, presumably in
an attempt to convert the vain
one to good conduct. Gentileschi
was the leading Roman follower
of Caravaggio.

Bernardo Strozzi

(Genoa 1581 – Venice 1644)

Tribute Money, c. 1630

Canvas, 159.5 x 123.5 cm – inv. no. 463 –
Acquired in 1711 for the Düsseldorf Gallery

Not until the 16th century is the theme of tribute due rendered in visual terms. "Give therefore to Cesar, the things which are Cesars, and give unto God, those things which are Gods" were Christ's words to the Pharisees when they wanted to trap him on the question of the legality of paying tribute to the Roman Emperor (Mat. 22, 15–21). His interlocutor is holding out a coin to him. Strozzi did eight variations on the theme. Seeing the work of Rubens, van Dyck and the Venetians had a noticeable impact on the Genoese painter's style.

Guido Reni

(Calvenzano 1575 – Bologna 1542)

The Assumption, 1642

Silk, 295 x 208 cm – inv. no. 446 –
From the Düsseldorf Gallery

Reni is the leading exponent of
Baroque painting in Bologna.
Painted the year he died, *The
Assumption* is distinguished by
light silvery tonality, balanced symmetrical composition and a dramatic approach to the subject
matter. This work exemplifies the
austere classical style favoured by
the artist from about 1630. It

was greatly appreciated in the 19th
century.

Silk as a support is highly un
usual. The painting was commissioned as early as 1631 for the high
altar of the church of the Brother-
hood of Santa Maria degli Angeli
in Spilamberto (Modena). The
angels bearing the Virgin up into
Heaven are a direct reference to
the patronage of the Church for
which it was painted. Serious
financial straits forced the parish to
sell the painting to an unknown
purchaser 19 years after it was
placed in the church.

Pietro da Cortona
(Cortona 1596 – Rome 1669)

Rest on the Flight into Egypt, c. 1643
Copper, 47.7 x 38.9 cm – inv. no. 176 –
From the Düsseldorf and Mannheim
Galleries

The painter's real name was Pietro Berrettini. Here he has configured the group in a classical triangular composition. Framed with foliation, it makes a monumental impact. An angel is proffering an apple to the Christ Child while, in the background, Joseph is returning from the fruitless search for lodging. The little painting was commissioned in 1639 by Cardinal Antonio Barberini, a relative of Urban VIII, who was then Pope. Cortona had just finished his masterpiece, the ceiling fresco glorifying this Pope in the Gran Salone of the Palazzo Barberini in Rome, which represents a landmark in Baroque decorative arts.

Giovanni Battista Pittoni
(Venice 1687 – Venice 1767)

The Birth of Christ, c. 1735
Canvas, 73.2 x 56 cm – inv. no. 5762 –
Acquired in 1812 from Bayreuth Castle

Numerous copies prove how popular this rendering of the subject was. Pittoni himself painted several versions of it. Its success is due to concentration on thematic essentials and appropriate qualities of atmosphere, with parerga reduced to indispensable elements. The cloudy background is mystically transfigured to underscore the miraculous quality of the event. Joseph's position in the foreground emphasizes the homely aspect of family life. The mother's gesture of showing her child includes the viewer in her tender solicitude. A major Italian Baroque painter, Pittoni played a decisive role in shaping Italian Rococo painting.

Canaletto (Giovanni Antonio Canal)
(Venice 1697 – Venice 1768)

St Mark's Square and Basin – Santa Maria della Salute and the Riva degli Schiavoni in Venice, c. 1740

Canvas, 69.1 x 94.5 cm and 69.7 x 94.5 cm – inv. nos. WAF 137, WAF 138 – Acquired by King Ludwig I from Canova's estate

The veduta or view of a real city-scape flourished in 18th-century Venice. It was overwhelmingly popular, not just with English upper-class youth on the "Grand Tour" with their tutors. When the War of the Austrian Succession (1740-48) left Canaletto bereft of clientele, he turned to drawing and etching. The two paintings shown here are companion pieces. Two others were sold in 1939. They exemplify the artist's austere, topographically accurate style marked by a cool, light palette and devoid of the chiaroscuro effects characteristic of his early work. Canaletto used a *camera obscura* (Lat. "dark chamber") to project the outlines so that he could trace them with precision.

Giovanni Battista Tiepolo

(Venice 1696 – Madrid 1770)

The Adoration of the Magi, 1753

Canvas, 408 x 210.5 cm – signed and dated – inv. no. 1159 – Acquired in 1804 during secularization

Tiepolo's oeuvre is regarded as the greatest achievement of Italian 18th-century painting. In 1750–1753 the artist worked in the Prince-Bishop's Palace in Würzburg. He may have painted *The Adoration of the Magi* for the high altar of Schwarzach Monastery church during the winter of 1752/53. Tiepolo knew how to stage a scene. Masterly handling of light and brilliant colour effects focus on the centre of the representation. The turbaned man and the kneeling page are a device leading into the composition encountered again in Tiepolo's frescoes.

Francesco Guardi
(Venice 1712 – Venice 1793)

Regatta on the Canale della Giudecca, c. 1784/89

Canvas, 61 x 93 cm – inv. no. HuW 34 –
Acquired in 1975, Bayerische Hypotheken-
und Wechselbank Collection

Guardi started out working in the manner of Canaletto's vedute although he always preferred freedom of handling to topographical accuracy. Effervescent colour laid on with rapid-fire brushwork to create dazzling light effects makes his work memorable. After the death of his brother Gianantonio in 1760, Francesco took over his studio and was able to develop his own distinctive style. His contemporaries criticized it and he was soon forgotten after his death. Not until the early 20th century and the success of Impressionism was Guardi's work appreciated as it deserves to be.

Starting in the east, this view of the city encompasses the Giudecca Canal, which extends to the horizon. The "wide-angle" effect (rather like 1960s photographs taken through a "fish-eye" lens) is a startling and, contrasted with Canaletto, innovative treatment of a panorama view. You feel you are seeing the earth's curvature. Dotted with gondolas and festively decorated boats which enhance the wide-angle effect, the Giudecca Canal runs into the Canal Grande on the right with the Customs House and the Church of Santa Maria della Salute. The painter's standpoint can be imagined as fairly high up and somewhere along the San Marco Canal. The painting shows how imaginatively Guardi set to work at achieving an original view of the city. Two drawings served as preliminary studies for the painting.

17th and 18th-Century French Painting

In the 17th century, Rome exerted a dominant influence on French painting. Poussin and Lorrain developed distinctively classical styles of their own while Valentin and Vouet were swept up in the prevailing currents of movements like Caravaggism. Others, like Bourdon, painted bambocciate (French bambochade) pictures in the manner of van Laer. Painting based on the principles espoused by the Académie Royale, founded in 1648, is represented in the Alte Pinakothek by Le Sueur. Most 17th-century French paintings in the museum once belonged to Wittelsbach collections. By contrast, the generous patronage of Munich banks has enabled the Alte Pinakothek to enlarge what was originally only a rudimentary collection of 18th-century French art. Boucher is represented with superbly showy pieces like the portrait of Mme de Pompadour and elegant scènes galantes based on mythological themes. Fragonard dealt with the latter deftly in an even more light-hearted manner marked by spontaneity of handling and playful characterization.

Nicolas Poussin

(Villers near Les Andelys 1594 – Rome 1665)

Midas and Bacchus, after 1624

Canvas, 98.5 x 153 cm – inv. no. 528 –
From the Kurfürstliche Galerie
(Prince Elector's Gallery)

The theme of metamorphosis derives from Ovid. Midas, King of Phrygia, guides Silenus, who has lost his way, back to Bacchus. The reward offered to Midas is a wish and he requests that everything he touches turn to gold. Nearly starving, Midas soon has to beg for release from this ill-chosen bounty. This is the moment depicted here. In the background Midas is kneeling on the river bank, washing himself clean as instructed by Bacchus. The water is stained gold.

The painting is an early Poussin, dating from the artist's first years in Rome from 1624. Revealed in the clarity with which he has arranged his figures, Poussin's classicism derives from thorough study of the High Renaissance and antiquity (see Rubens' *Drunken Silenus,* p. 78).

Nicolas Poussin

(Villers near Les Andelys 1594 –
Rome 1665)

The Lamentation, c. 1627

Canvas, 102.7 x 146.1 – inv. no. 625 – From
the Kurfürstliche Galerie (Prince Elector's
Gallery)

The scene has been depicted with
archaeological precision. Joseph of
Arimathaea, a "man of means",
had a chamber grave built like the
one on the right and then had the
body of Christ placed in it (Mat. 27,
57-60). In his arrangement of figures, Poussin has reverted to the
Renaissance ideal of the triangular
composition, transposing it to an
elongated landscape format. A brilliant colourist, Poussin has built
up a sombre mood around the
stark tonality of the reddish grey
rock. Touches of icy blue, brilliant
red and clear white are in sharp
contrast.

Sébastien Bourdon

(Montpellier 1616 – Paris 1671)

Roman Lime-Kiln, c. 1634/37

Canvas, 172 x 246 cm – inv. no. 155 –
From the Kurfürstliche Galerie
(Prince Elector's Gallery)

Bourdon painted this scene during
a four-year stay in Rome, where he
went at eighteen. It combines the
genre of the veduta or view of the
city (you can spot the Tomb of Cae
cilia Metella and Castel Sant' Ange-
lo) with the genre scenes of Roman
street life made popular by the
Dutch painter Pieter van Laer, who
is credited with inventing them.
They are called *bambocciate* (bam-
boccio means "little clumsy one",
an allusion to van Laer's diminu-
tive size and deformity). From the
Middle Ages, Rome was dotted
with such kilns, in which many an
ancient marble column was
reduced to lime.

Claude Le Lorrain
(Chamagne near Mirecourt 1600 – Rome 1682)

The Banishment of Hagar – Hagar and Ishmael in the Wilderness, 1668

Canvas, 106.5 x 140.3 cm and 106.4 x 140 cm – signed and dated – inv. nos. 604 and 598 – Once owned by the director of the Zweibrücken Gallery, Johann Christian von Mannlich

After Isaac's birth Abraham yielded to the wish of his wife Sarah and banished the Egyptian bondwoman Hagar and Ishmael, his son by Hagar (Gen. 21, 9-21), giving them only bread and water as provisions. Sarah is maliciously observing the scene from the balcony. In the companion piece, an angel rescues Hagar and Ishmael from dying of thirst in the desert by showing them a spring. Both paintings are serene in mood. After all, this is happening with God's permission. He intended to found a great people descended from both Isaac (Sarah's son) and Ishmael. Viewed as if from a plateau, the ideal landscape is sweeping in its breadth. The pervasive tonal value of silvery light creates the atmosphere of these pieces. The two paintings are related to each other by framing landscape elements. Born in Lorraine ("Le Lorrain"), Claude Gellée went to Rome at the age of twelve. He spent almost his whole life there, greatly admired as a landscape painter. Most of his work is assured since he recorded it from 1635 in a "Liber veritatis". The pair of Hagar paintings was commissioned by Johann Friedrich, Count Waldstein, Archbishop of Prague.

Claude Le Lorrain

(Chamagne near Mirecourt 1600 – Rome 1682)

Harbour at Dawn, 1674

Canvas, 72.2 x 96 cm – signed and dated – Inv. no. 381 – From the Kurfürstliche Galerie (Prince Elector's Gallery)

This painting is the companion piece to *Idyllic Landscape at Sunset*, (not reproduced here) executed four years previously. In both, the enchantment of light recreates the mood and atmosphere of the time of day. The two paintings were commissioned for the Bavarian Electoral Councilman, Franz von Mayer in Regensburg.

Nicolas Lancret
(Paris 1690 – Paris 1745)

The Birdcage, c. 1735

Canvas, 44 x 48 cm – inv. no. HuW 4 –
Acquired in 1966, Bayerische Hypotheken-
und Wechselbank Collection

The charm of this painting lies in
evocative symbolism and sophisticated colouring. Playing with birds,
whether in cages or released to fly
about, had erotic connotations, particularly when associated with pastoral themes. The large number of
reproductions of this motif as
copperplate engravings or even
on objets de vertu proves that
Lancret's idea was to generalize the
subject. The painting was once in
the collection of Frederick the
Great at Potsdam.

Jean Baptiste Chardin
(Paris 1699 – Paris 1799)

Woman Peeling Turnips, c. 1740

Canvas, 46 x 37 cm – signed – inv. no.
1090 – From the Zweibrücken Gallery

Chardin's work evokes moods like
serenity and concentration and is
distinguished by consummate
technique. Known for representations of working people as well as
still lifes, he always captures
moments of repose in the hustle
and bustle of workaday life. The
viewer is caught up in the contem-
plative mood of these works. A
master of genre with an emphasis
on "kitchen scenes", he takes up
where Dutch genre painting left
off in the 17th century. However,
his motifs are drawn from French
lower middle-class life.

Jean Etienne Liotard
(Geneva 1702 – Geneva 1789)

Breakfast, c. 1745

Pastel on vellum, 61 x 51 cm – inv. no.
HuW 30 – Acquired in 1974, Bayerische
Hypotheken- und Wechselbank Collection

Pastels were known as a medium
by the 15th and 16th centuries.
However, they did not become
fashionable until the Rococo period, when the delicate colour and
slightly powdery surface finish of
pastel paintings seems to have
had a particular appeal. Fabric
textures could be rendered with
exquisite delicacy in pastel. Here
Liotard has combined portraiture
and genre painting. Cutting off

the figure on the left as he has
done here was a bold stroke
indeed.

François Boucher
(Paris 1703 – Paris 1770)

Reclining Girl, 1752

Canvas, 59 x 72.9 cm – signed and dated – inv. no. 1166 – From the Zweibrücken Gallery

The girl depicted here is probably Louise O'Murphy at fifteen. She worked from 1751 as a model for Boucher and after Louis XV had seen a miniature of her in 1753, he made her his mistress. She bore a child and was subsequently married to Jacques de Beaufranchet in 1755. The piquant blend of childlike naivety and overtly erotic pose which Boucher has presented here so appetisingly represents the quintessence of playful sexuality in a frivolous age.

François Boucher
(Paris 1703 – Paris 1770)

Portrait of Mme de Pompadour, 1756

Canvas, 201 x 157 cm – signed and dated – inv. no. HuW 18 – Acquired in 1971, Bayerische Hypotheken- und Wechselbank Collection

Four years after her marriage to Charles-Guillaume Le Normant d'Etioles in 1745, Jeanne-Antoinette Poisson became the mistress of Louis XV. The king greatly admired her intellect and musical talent and she soon rose to an elevated position at court, culminating in her appointment as a Lady-in-Waiting (*dame du palais*) to the Queen on 7 February 1756. Probably commissioned to commemorate this occasion, the painting is both an intimate likeness and an official state portrait.

Mme de Pompadour is dressed for court and surrounded by objects which allude to her skills and interests. The book on her lap underscores her literary erudition. The letter, pen and seal on the little desk recall her polished epistolary style. The sheets of music and engravings (one of them from her own hand after Boucher's work) represent a casual tribute to her musical and artistic leanings. In front of her is her favourite King Charles spaniel, Mimi. The large mirror behind the sofa extends the picture space. The painting may well have been executed in Boucher's studio from hand and head studies. The sumptuous cascade of silken folds was probably painted from a model wearing the magnificent dress. François Boucher, painter, draughtsman and engraver, was the most versatile of French Rococo artists. At the Versailles court he was greatly appreciated for his mastery of decoration in all details.

Jean Honoré Fragonard
(Grasse 1732 – Paris 1806)

Girl with a Lap-Dog (La Gimblette),
c. 1770

Canvas, 89 x 70 cm – inv. no. HuW 35 –
Acquired in 1977, Bayerische Hypotheken-
und Wechselbank Collection

Both sketchy and in places deliberately unfinished, the execution is
as playful as the motif. The lascivi-
ous goings-on with her lap-dog
indulged in by the girl, who thinks
she is unobserved, shocked even
hardened contemporaries of the
painter's. The title attached to the
piece, *La Gimblette*, was really that
of another painting.

Chardin and Boucher were
Fragonard's teachers. The painter's
origins were Milanese. During the
French Revolution, Fragonard's
work was banned and the painter
died in obscurity.

16th and 17th-Century Spanish Painting

The Spanish section is numerically the smallest collection in the Alte Pinakothek. Nevertheless, all the great names are there: El Greco, Velázquez, Zurbarán and Murillo. During the 16th and 17th centuries, Spanish painting went its own way in European art because most of it was commissioned by either the Court or the Church. Court portraits and religious paintings are, therefore, strongly represented here. Mythological themes and moralizing content, popular in Flemish and other major European painting, were not fashionable in Spain. Genre painting, too, was only of minor importance there. Nearly all of Murillo's moving genre scenes were sold abroad. The Alte Pinakothek collection of Spanish paintings is largely 17th-century. Strange as it may seem, this was the age that saw the flowering of Spanish culture, even while Spain was declining as a political and economic global power. Most of these paintings came to Munich from 17th and 18th-century Wittelsbach collections.

Juan Pantoja de la Cruz
(Valladolid 1553 – Madrid 1608)

Portrait of the Infanta Isabella Clara Eugenia, 1599

Canvas, 124.7 x 97.5 cm – signed and dated – inv. no. 987 – Acquired from the Benedictine convent at Hohenwart in 1804 during secularization

The Infanta was the daughter of Philip II. Her father entrusted her with governing the Netherlands after her marriage to Grand Duke Albrecht VII of Austria, a son of the Emperor Maximilian II. Its companion piece (inv. no. 898) is not reproduced here. The austerity and constraints of Spanish court ceremony are expressed in this portrait. The heaviness of the dress, weighted down with jewels, is what hits the eye even more than its sumptuousness. The pose and even the royal sitter's gesture of fingering her rope of pearls look hieratic.

Diego Rodriguez de Silva y Velázquez
(Seville 1599 – Madrid 1660)

Portrait of a Spanish Nobleman, c. 1629

Canvas, 89.2 x 69.5 cm – inv. no. 518 – Acquired for the Düsseldorf Gallery in 1694

The portrait is unfinished. The hands are only indicated by a contour sketch in broad, black brush strokes. The sitter's doublet has been laid on without any further modulation. Finally, the background has not been finished around the figure, where the light brown ground shines through. Perhaps its unfinished state is what creates the immediacy of this portrait. The face of the unknown young man seems to jump out at you in its three-dimensionality. The sitter wears Spanish Court dress in the style fashionable after Philip IV ascended the throne. By then a flat, starched collar (golilla) had replaced the broad ruff.

El Greco
(Fodele near Candia 1541 – Toledo 1614)

Christ Stripped of His Garments,
c. 1606/08

Canvas, 165 x 98.8 cm – inv. no. 8573 –
Acquired in 1909 on the French art market

As a young man, Doménikos Theotokópoulos, known as El Greco, was an icon painter in his native Crete. In 1566 he moved to Venice, where he trained in Titian's workshop. Tintoretto and Bassano exerted a formative influence on him.

From 1577 he worked in Toledo, Spain. El Greco's art represents a unique synthesis of hieratic Byzantine painting, Venetian handling of colour and Mannerist principles of composition and rendering of figures. Attenuated figures and flat groupings alternating with exaggerated spatial depth, extreme chiaroscuro and colour contrasts are the salient features of his style. This is a replica from the artist's own hand of the work he executed for the sacristy of Toledo Cathedral in 1577/79.

Francisco de Zurbarán y Salazar
(Fuente de Cantos 1598 – Madrid 1664)

The Entombment of St Catherine of Alexandria on Mt Sinai, after 1630

Canvas, 201.5 x 126 cm – inv. no. 14933 –
Acquired in 1985 from a private collection

After she was beheaded, the saint was taken by angels to Mt Sinai, where she was buried. Here the angels are about to lower the corpse into the sarcophagus. On the right the instruments of torture are depicted. This altarpiece prob-ably came from St Catherine's chapel in the church of the Merce-darian mendicant order in Seville, consecrated in 1636. As in other, similarly structured compositions, the upper quarter of the picture plane is sketchy in execution. The handling becomes increasingly precise towards the lower third, culminating in stringently ren-dered, cool pink and grey fabric textures. Here Zurbarán was work-ing after an engraving by Cornelis Cort (1575).

Bartholomé Esteban Murillo
(Seville 1618 – Seville 1682)

Beggar Boys Eating Grapes and Melons, c. 1645/46

Canvas, 145.9 x 103.6 cm – inv. no. 605 –
Probably acquired in 1698 by the Prince
Elector Max Emanuel

Murillo is famous for his moving genre scenes and emotional religious paintings. His rendering of the "Immaculate Conception" shaped the typology of that motif. Sold by art dealers on the European market during the 17th century, Murillo's genre paintings are still all outside Spain. Children, particularly beggar children, captured in what purport to be scenes from daily life, are the subject of his genre pictures. The appeal of these works lies paradoxically in their ideal quality. None of these urchins looks hungry and all are bursting with health. What makes Murillo's genre scenes so touching or even sweet is really clever staging. Not even tattered clothing is pitiful here because it has been rendered with such slick virtuosity. Careful treatment of light enhances the plasticity of the figures.

Bartholomé Esteban Murillo

(Seville 1618 – Seville 1682)

Urchins Playing Dice, c. 1675

Canvas, 146 x 108 cm – inv. no. 597 –
Acquired by the Prince Elector Max
Emanuel in 1698

The other four Murillo genre paintings in Munich were painted three
decades after *Beggar Boys Eating
Grapes and Melons*. This was the
earliest of them. The pale light
flooding the picture plane may really reflect light conditions in Seville
alleys, which have always been covered over with awnings to keep out
the heat of the sun. Perhaps it is
siesta time here. The little boy gazing so dreamily out of the picture
was used by Murillo as the model
for a Cherub in his representations
of the Immaculate Conception.

Index of Artists